# Options Trading Crash Course

*How to Make Strategic Investments with Consistent Daily Returns that 95% of New Traders Fail to Make. Suitable for Beginners and More Experienced Traders*

**By**

**Jim Norton**

# Introduction

People exchange options on the stock market to gain from currency movements. That is, to make money from trades, investors use the low buy and high sell strategy.

You can buy options that expire on various dates. Almost all of the activity focuses on options expiring within a week or a month. Some options expire in the distant future, for example, in several weeks or months, and even years.  As we will see, the options' expiry date is something that you will need to be very careful indeed.

However, for new investors, one of the best things about options is the high return on investment or ROI!

Therefore, because of the low investment amounts required to get started, trading of options is far more accessible than trading stocks for a day or the swing trading practice, and you will earn much higher returns!

To be successful in trading, it takes hard work and a lot of research. This concept applies not only to option trading but also to all other financial activities. Be mindful of time intervals when trading options, and remember that you will not see any dramatic changes in the price of your options within the first few weeks or a few months. The reason for this is that the trading profit comes from the losses of other traders. The method of generating profit is the same if you swap derivatives, stocks, or options. When you reduce the fees that dealers and brokers take, it will decrease the number of funds that go around.  These amounts of money are another reason why so many operators struggle during the trade. You should train yourself to avoid the fate of many of these brokers. Learn how and when to trade more intelligently, as it will allow you to succeed or, at worst, to survive in the trading market.

Consider this book clearly as the beginning of your options trading journey. You can grasp the basic terms and methods for your future career and recognize them. It should provide you with the foundation you need and encourage you to care for yourself and educate yourself further.

Several low constraints on entry-trading occupations have resulted from technical developments and rising exchange rates. In some cases, no additional capital is needed. In contrast, in other cases, to validate your commercial purpose, only a small amount of capital is required to get you going. With markets so interconnected, somewhere across the globe, there is still free trade time. Many markets can be reached with relative ease, which implies that even people with full-time jobs or jobless people at home can trade. It is all about having the right chance and demand.

This book has been written for anyone who wants to begin trading options and learn the trading art. This book contains all the vital data one requires to become a profitable trader. You will note how this book will shift your outlook on trading options once you start reading this book and that trading options are not as complicated as individuals make it seem. It is all about the right preparations and tactics, and you are ready to go!

## Chapter 1: Basics of Options Trading

Trading options is much like trading stocks, though there are significant differences. There are two major categories of options (calls and puts): agreements that grant the bearer the fundamental right, such as a stock, to buy or sell the underlying security. However, options are traded on exchanges just as stocks are. Individual investors may use a brokerage company to place buying and selling requests.

Options are precious as they can improve an individual's portfolio. By adding income, offering power, and even protection, they do so. Usually, there is a selection of options tailored to an investor's interest, depending on the situation. A more straightforward instance would be to use options as an effective defense against a weakening stock market to mitigate downside risks. Options may also be used to produce recurring revenue. Sometimes, they are used for hypothetical purposes, including making bets on the direction of the stock.

It is not unusual to invest in options. The first options contract, in reality, debuted in 1973 on the Chicago Board Options Exchange. Although today's option is still close to what it was, a lot has changed. The company size in terms of creditors, exchange rates, and exchange contracts is the most crucial distinction; this has grown exponentially. More trading options are now available than ever.

Investors use options for particular purposes. Mainly, a call option is a contract granting the holder the right to purchase a stock at a defined price for a specific period. If they expect a more drastic change in the share price, some investors buy calls. Others will sell calls if a stock price is anticipated to flat-trade or to shift lower.

You need to learn what they are first to trade options. An option is a contract related to a specific stock or other investment between a buyer and a seller. The option buyer has the right to compel the option seller within the time-limit set by the agreement to do as the contract specifies. The seller must meet the option's instructions until the buyer has exercised the option.

The options adhere to the broader group of securities classified as derivatives. A derivative's value depends on or is determined from something else's value. A stock option is a stock derivative. Options are financial equity derivatives; their value depends on the price of some other asset. Calls, Puts, Options, Forwards, Swaps, and Mortgage-backed securities, among others, are examples of derivatives.

## 1.1 What is Options Trading?

Options are agreements that grant the bearer the right, and not the duty, to either sell or buy the sum of any underlying asset at a fixed price at or before the contract's expiry. Options may be purchased from mutual investment accounts, like any other asset class.

Investors necessitate brokerage accounts to invest in people who expect that their original investment will turn into life-changing wealth for the stock. But it's essential to select a broker that gives you direct exposure to all the different kinds of exciting investments. While most brokers will meet basic needs, those who want to take advantage of advanced investment strategies need to be careful in choosing brokers who can give them the opportunity to trade and the resources they need in those areas to make the right options.

Stock options are not as difficult as people would make them seem. People tend to make it sound complex at times, but it is a simple thing that almost everyone can understand. Do not stop yourself as a novice from thinking that trading options are an emotional investment. You'd be surprised at how simple and straightforward it is and wonder why you've never invested in it before. There are four factors which investors should consider when investing in stock options. To take account of these factors, this would have a positive effect on their trade.

One chance to turn the trade is to look at the options market. Trading options are very different from trading mutual funds or bonds, but they can have many enormous advantages for investors. Below, you can look at precisely what trading options are and how they can benefit you.

The most significant thing regarding an option is that the buyer of an option has the power to pursue the contract, as its name implies, but is under no pressure to do so. Hence, only if it is wise to do so, the Buyer of Option can use this right. Assume in the following example that the Call Option allowed the buyer to pay $200 per share for a specific stock. Suppose the stock is sold on the open market for $100 a share. In that case, the option holder will never exercise the option since it would be dumb to pay $200 on the free market under the promise of a share that the buyer might purchase for $100. However, if the market share price was $275, then the buyer could exercise the right, as $200 would be a steal over the share price commonly owned.

For example, a stock call option provides the buyer of the option the right to purchase a specific number of shares at a given price at any time before the stated expiry date. If the buyer exercises the right, the seller of the option must sell the stock to the buyer.

Amongst those top picks for you, find the best stockbroker. There's a stockbroker to meet your business needs if you are looking for an exclusive sign-up offer, excellent customer service, $0 commissions, intuitive smartphone applications, or more.

There are several different trading options. In addition to the call options stated above, put options give the buyer option the right to sell stock at a given price, thus protecting the buyer option from stock losses. To take advantage of more sophisticated approaches to options that can make a profit in various cases, you can also combine various call and put options.

A contract that gives the investor the right to sell or buy an asset at a fixed agreed strike price at a specified date depending on the form of option, while not an obligation, we can quickly identify stock options now that we know the definition of both stocks and options. We may describe the term as follows: stock options offer an owner the right at a given price and date to sell or buy a stock.

The stock option may also refer to an incentive in the form of an opportunity offered by a business to any employee to buy shares in a company at a predetermined fixed price or a discount.

Stock options have become a source of concern in recent years. We are seeing more and more individuals interested in options for trading. Some think it's a scam; others say it's not a worthwhile investment, while others say it's not a worthwhile investment. All these speculations lead us in one direction, namely, understanding what stock options are. We are going to have to go over stock options very carefully to answer this question correctly. We'll need to know more about it and what it means. This experience makes it simpler, instead of using theories, to make decisions with facts. You should never back up something you will get to tell you. Having awareness gives you an added value and puts you in the right spot.

Knowledge gathering will alter your trading skills as an inexperienced trader. It will make you an expert in the trade to acquire the necessary abilities and knowledge within a matter of time. Before you commit to a stock option, this book will give you the information you need. It is nice that you have taken the first step towards getting this book. It demonstrates that you are ready and eager to know, and that is a big step. Learning to apply it is essential; apart from gaining skills, you will do what you have learned. Most individuals receive data but are unable to make successful use of it for their benefit. In addition to acquiring expertise, having to learn to apply is necessary. It is going to mean doing what you heard. Many individuals collect data but are unable to make equal use of it for their benefit. We hope you will have the courage to trade a stock option after you read the book. The book focuses on beginners in particular and is intended to make a difference in their lives.

## 1.2 The Options Jargons

Being familiar with Options Trading needs some vocabulary to remember. The basics for starting up to trade options are here.

**Strike Price:**

The strike price would have to be calculated to know whether a stock could be exercised. When an alternative arrives at the expiry date, there is a meaning that it is expected to have; this may be lower or higher than the stock price, which we refer to as the strike price of an associated asset. You can buy a Call Option at a fixed price for the strike if you expect the investment cost to rise as an investor. The value of a call will become the price beyond which the holder of the option will sell an asset if the bid expires when placing calls. Maybe the strike price, too, will be the exercise price. It is a crucial aspect to recognize when assessing the significance of the alternative. Depending on when the options are exercised, the strike price may vary. As an investor, it is a great approach to keep watching the strike price to explain its success.

**The Right, but Not the Liability:**

What comes to mind immediately when this sentence is being read? Yeah, we say that you can purchase any product when we talk or have rights. We refer to the fact that one has no legal authority to perform an obligation when we speak about responsibility. Options do not grant a lawful right to perform a mission to traders, this indicates that the right of trade is there, but the statute does not enforce it.

**Contracts:**
Contracts refer to the number of shares required to be purchased by individuals. An asset class of one hundred shares corresponds to a contract. When determining the value of the stock before the expiry date, contracts ought to be dignified. After the expiry date, a contract can be counted as void. Understanding this will allow you to find the right moment to work out a contract. For a case in which somebody buys ten options, an investor gets ten calls for $350. Suppose stock prices go past $ 350 at the expiry rate. In that case, the dealer receives an opportunity to buy or sell 1000 stock shares at $ 350: this occurs at the same moment, regardless of the stock's price. The option expires uselessly in a situation where the stock is below $350. That will result in a complete loss as an investor. You will lose the whole amount you used to buy the options, and you will not get it back. Be aware of the contracts and exercise them on outstanding trading results if you consider engaging in trading options.

**The Date of Expiration:**
The expiry date refers to the period during which a contract is declared null. Stocks have an expiration date. The time between the period they were bought, and the expiry date indicates an option's validity. As a trader, you are required to use the contracts for your benefit during this time. As much as you can over the sales period, you can sell over the expiry period and earn high returns. Discover how to make equal use of the available time. The right will expire before you are given a chance to exercise it if you are not cautious.

We will have starters who participate in this aspect and progressively lose eventually. It would require you to be careful about trying to invest in the stock market. Your securities would be considered worthless without an opportunity to invest in them if you fail to check the expiry date. Stock, in certain unusual cases, are exercised before the expiry date.

**Price set:**
There is the same price bundle for the right to exercise. The cost can vary according to the product type. It seems that individual stock options are more lucrative than others. Multiple variables calculate option rates. These points will come through to you as you keep reading this book. Depending on the variables' effect, knowing them will help you understand when and how to conduct a trade or not make a trade; a trade will yield a high profit or lead to a loss.

**Premium:**
The premium refers to the cash you use to buy options. By multiplying by 100, the cost of a call, and the number of agreements, you get the bonus. The '100' displays the number of shares per deal: this is a lot about the trader's investment expected to produce substantial returns. You should expect the venture in which you have chosen to participate in producing profitable results when investing. In industry, nobody expects a loss. You believe like one is still optimistic that the investment they have chosen to engage in will benefit them. All you look forward to is using an arrangement to its full benefit.

You are going to learn about different ideas as you decide to invest. Don't let your words frighten you; you knew that you were mostly packed with them, but you did not know they were going by that name. Many individuals overspend on inventories, mainly because the different words used are difficult to comprehend. The situation should not be this. It would be better to take a little time, go over the words, and grasp what they mean thoroughly.

**Styles:**

Two basic types are vital. There are options in the American and European models. If you want to share options, educating yourself in different ways is helpful. When you compare the templates to those that don't, you will know those that work for you. You can often find that it is easier to grasp and handle a particular model than others. You may want to take part in the easy thing for you and avoid taking part in the one you have difficulty understanding.

Any date between the moment of acquisition and the expiry of a contract to be traded provides the American-style option. Most traders participate in this style due to its ease. Any period during which a transaction is deemed valid involves the execution of a trade.

The European Style Option is not widely used in contrast with the American style. Only in the European Option format may a trader exercise his options during the expiry period. Experts warn people not to consider the European form if individuals are not Options Trading experts.

**Purchase or Sale:**

You are granted the right to buy or swap an option as a seller. There are two kinds of inventories that one can pick from. We have the chance to be put, as well as the opportunity to call. They both vary, and each has its advantages and disadvantages.

**Contract Expiry:**

The expiration date is when it is assumed that a contract is void. Stock Options have an expiry date. The year is defined for the calculation of the value of the option. Correspondence is believed to be correct at any point before the expiry date, and this means that it can be used at any stage before the expiry date to generate revenue. When it hits the expiry date, a dealer has no right to practice the law. That is because the agreement is perceived to be null. As an investor, this is necessary during its time of validity to ensure that your investment is correct.

## 1.3 Options Trading vs. Conventional Trading Methods

While stocks attract long-term investors and students, for skilled traders who value flexibility, options can work well. Both metaphorically and literally, you have options when taking stock on how to invest in the market.

Stocks are individual company ownership shares, while alternatives are agreements with several other investors that allow you to bet on the way you think a stock price is going. These assets can be matched in a portfolio. Still, there are significant variations between stocks and options, and investors compatible with both of them.

One thing to bear in mind is that it may sound thrilling to discover incredibly lucrative investments within the equity or options markets. Even, you would need to take into account low-cost equity funds as well as exchange-traded funds before you plunge into options trading or day trading. These instruments combine various assets (such as shares or bonds) to allow you to extend your portfolio even from a single investment. Experts also recommend investors use these funds to form the base of a long-term portfolio, which may act as a start-up investor entry point.

**Options Trading Vs. Stock Trading**

If you aim to look for a simple way to start investing over five years for a goal, such as a pension, stocks might be the right option. Since there is no guarantee that you can make money, any individual stock's production can be unpredictable. The corresponding investment period is typically shorter concerning options, making them especially attractive to traders who actively buy and sell. Expiry dates, which may range from weeks to years, occur with all option contracts. If you trade options or stocks, here is a quick glimpse into what you will get.

**Stocks**

The essence of investing is simplicity: you buy a stock, expecting its value to rise so that at some point, you can sell at a higher price. If you plan to hold a stock for years at least or try your hand at day-to-day trading, this refers to buying and vigorously selling stocks over short timeframes such as days or weeks.

Stocks are a traditional entry point into the stock market for start-up investors, particularly people who have a long-term strategy. They are more manageable, appear to have relatively lower costs, and allow for a straightforward approach.

You want to invest in after discovering the stocks, and you don't need to obsessively watch them every day, those you truly believe have a growth potential that suits your timeframes as well. Until you need the money or set a particular alarm to warn you when the stock price hits the amount you wish to sell through your online broker, you can keep an eye on them.

The stock-related risk is very straightforward: it means the price could fall, and as the individual stock products can be volatile, most or all of your money will be lost daily. Usually, experts suggest investing in stocks for at least four or five years with the money you would not use. Usually, it is best to avoid throwing all your capital into one stock to reduce risk further.

Also, how actively you trade stocks can influence productivity and how much you will spend on profits in fees, commissions, and taxes. Stock trading commissions differ, but many online brokers have withdrawn them altogether. So, search around before setting up an account. Your capital gains tax rate is primarily based on whether you know the stock's sale value, how long you own it, taxes, and the higher earnings for shares holding for less than one year.

## Options

Are you looking for a more insightful investment plan, one with reduced capital conditions and flexibility in the timing or future losses? There could be optioned up your alley.

The corresponding period of the investment is typically shorter for options, making them more viable for traders who actively make trades. There are expiry dates for all selection agreements, which can vary from weeks to years.

The investment method creates complexity, but many people enjoy the flexibility provided by alternatives, namely the opportunity to see how trading works and lock in a cost without a purchasing commitment. You need to make three instead of enforcing one move, like betting whether or not the price of a stock will go up:

- The direction of the stock movement
- How low or high it can fly from its current price
- The period that it will occur throughout

The above is about trading options at their simplest; seasoned traders have far more complex techniques.

Trading Options provides an opportunity in a detailed vocabulary to learn words such as calls, puts, and strike rates, which may make you think that those assets are more volatile than stocks. In particular, since investors are prepared to allow an option to expire and do not assume any additional financial obligation, except the premium and the trading costs charged, this definition can be overstated. Long-term investors could also use options as their tool for hedging. For example, buying a Put Option could help mitigate losses if the value of the stock you own goes down.

Trading options require a more realistic approach than trading in stocks. Before expiry, you will decide to exercise the particular option, which implies that you will have to keep an eye on the stock price. Alerts from your online broker can also be set up.

Some option strategies are much riskier than others. Make sure you know the trade beforehand. Many analysts suggest that daily or weekly options, which appear to be a better fit for experienced traders, should be avoided.

The related rates, which could be considerably higher than they are for stocks, are another downside of Options Trading. Options traders will also pay a fixed fee per bid that, whether one is paid, is the same as the broker's stock trading fee, plus a fee ranging from 15 cents to 75 cents per contract. Consequently, the more you trade, the higher your expenses are, and do not forget, you can also pay sales fees. Make sure you factor back capital gains income, as with stocks. You will have to pay the earnings taxes; these taxes are far higher on the assets that you have owned for less than a year.

Lastly, depending on your investing style, it is a personal matter to decide which strategy is suitable for you. In general, inexperienced investors and investors who prefer the ease of access will turn to stocks because of their simple character — exchange options may attract investors who want an aggressive trading strategy and love to watch the market

But don't presume that you have one commodity to rely on. Options traders, whether they exercise Call Options, ultimately become stock owners. Some stock traders have been using Put Options to test their hedging technique.

Options Trading is only for you if you are a committed and active investor and possess what it takes to be a profitable trader. Then obviously, you are not afraid of the risks.

**Options Trading Vs. Forex Trading**

You engage in contracts that, when trading options, may move stocks, index items, or ETFs (Exchange-Traded Fund). When betting on Forex, you try to profit from varying currency rates. Currency traders are also used in combinations, with a broker comparing the value between two reference currencies, such as the Dollar and the Euro. Both platforms have the chances of significant benefits, but which one is explicitly tailored for your financial plans and your risk appetite? Keep reading to grasp some of the critical features of each investment platform.

**Market Access:**

The Forex market is generally open. There is virtually always time to change with access to the market 24 hours a day, five days a week. The weekend markets are still technically open, but weekend trading is something that most Forex traders resist. The market for options is linked to the stock exchange, but trade is essentially limited to regular trading hours. (From 9 am until 4:30 pm); this can allow a trader to "intellectually switch off." However, it also prevents intelligent investors from reacting rapidly to market trends or current affairs that can present an investment opportunity.

**Quick Trades:**

It is all simple with Forex. When conducting Forex trades, everything happens almost instantly. Transactions are instantly focused, without gaps that have become common in options transactions or many other markets; this also implies that you can check your order at the price you want without dealing with any of the price slippages that options traders are famous for. When it comes to the trading rate, Forex has a distinct benefit.

**Leverage:**

Leverage is a fundamental idea that can make a big difference in terms of the opportunity for profit. It needs to be handled prudently to reduce over-exposure and significant risks. Leverage levels for currency trading can range from 50 to about 400 times the original investment. In contrast, option-related leverage ratios are often lower; this means that Forex traders can make substantially higher returns in a short time, all with a lower initial investment. However, to avoid disastrous effects, the leveraged asset needs to be tightly monitored. The message here is to start small and gradually lift leveraged positions.

**Commissions:**

Bear in mind that you might usually pay a fee to a broker each time you conduct a trade-in option. On the other hand, Forex trading operates inside a market that is a group of traders and devices that create a network that bypasses marketplace norms; this implies that you can miss fees by negotiating via Forex, but the Forex brokerage firm will gain money by applying a difference between the bid and the requested amount. That is where they can make their money. The good news is that the Forex model does not result in costs or commissions such as options trading, even though you have to pay slightly more than the baseline currency cost.

**Risk Management:**

Which business strategy provides the edge as it relates to risk management? The chosen strategy shows the trader you are and how you want the game to be pursued. Forex traders can also enforce position limits. If the margin sum outweighs the brokerage account's cost in dollars, the online trading system will automatically produce a margin call; this gives the trader an automatic safeguard that ensures that losses are kept under control. Remember that you can always determine the duration of time between Forex trades. At the same time, options only have a fixed trading period until the options expire.

Trading options can pose some apparent benefits for today's proactive traders. The global market is controlled closely, which means that a correctly understood and concrete marketplace helps to quench any ambiguity about the customer on the other end of a transaction. Gains can also be rendered above, below, and sideways in most of the market conditions. A centralized price also helps keep things stable. Options, however, can only be traded from Monday to Friday during "standard working hours, so that the seasoned investor is sitting around and watching his or her investment doing almost nothing."

Forex trading enables a trader with little upfront capital to open an account and start making financial decisions. Simple diversity is also possible when traders use micro or mini-batches of the exchange rate and retain financial leverage within reason. Markets are usually open 24 hours a day during the average week, and weekend trades are also possible. Still, most trading groups do not support them.

Bear in mind that the ability to conduct trades 24 hours a day can be seen as a benefit for many when deciding which possibility is better for you, but it may also lead to complications. Those who have a hard time segregating instinct from decent trade sense could find themselves over-trading due to the readily available market. Most investors want to make a purchase and then leave immediately, without having to worry at all times of the day about the state of their investments.

## Trading of Options vs. Day Trading

In financial markets, day trading and binary options, although they are separate species, are both factors that make or lose money. A binary option is mostly a kind of option wherein the impact of a yes or no market proposal is based solely on your profit/loss: a binary options trader will make either a fixed gain or a fixed loss. On the other hand, day-trading is a trading style where positions are opened or closed within the same trading period. A day trader's gain or loss depends on different variables, namely, the exit price, the entry price, and the number of contracts, shares, or lots purchased and sold by the trader.

An option is a monetary component that gives the buyer the right, but just not the responsibility, to buy or sell a fixed number of a security or other financial instrument at an agreed amount, on or before a specified date (the strike price). However, a binary option is automatically exercised, so the buyer will not have the option to buy or sell the asset.

Many underlying assets are available with binary options, including inventories, currencies, commodities, indices, and even operations, such as upcoming Fed Funds Pace, Jobless Claims, etc. A binary choice asks a yes/no query: at 1:00 pm, for example, will the price of gold be more than $1,250? If you feel yes, you buy a binary option, and you think no, you sell it. The price at which you purchase or sell the binary option is an actual value between zero and 100 instead of the actual price of gold (in this instance). The trading range keeps changing throughout the day, but either 100 (if the answer to that is yes) or zero is still settled (If no is the answer). The trader's profit or loss is calculated using the distinction between closing prices (null or 100) and the opening price (the price you bought or sold).

Binary options traders "place a bet" on whether the asset price would be lower or higher than a certain number at a given time or not. Often, day traders try to forecast the course of markets. Even so, gains and losses vary depending on the starting price, exit value, size of the trade, and financial management techniques. Day traders can use profit goals and stop losses go into a transaction anticipating maximum gains and losses, much more like binary options investors. For example, a day trader could enter a transaction and set a target profit of $250 and a stop loss of $70. Day traders, however, will let the profits run to reap the benefits of significant price movements. Of course, day traders can also let their losses get out of control by not using stop losses or hanging on a trade, hoping that it would change direction. A range of tools are purchased and sold by day traders, including currencies, stocks, indices, futures, commodities, and ETFs Exchange-Traded Fund.

## Chapter 2: How Does Options Trading Work?

Anyone willing to enter the domain of trading options should have a firm grasp of the principles and understanding of Options Trading's basic functionality, as Options Trading requires an individual to be well educated and willing to offer in the effort needed for the venture. This chapter will give you an overview of what Option Trading is and how it operates.

## 2.1 Understanding the Options Trading Mechanism

In a trade, several players are involved. Trading directly with others is not feasible, and it is not even realistic. Stock exchanges were developed for usability; this is a network where all stocks are shared.

Because this will cause significant uncertainty, you should not negotiate with the stock exchange directly. So many individuals will be making deals simultaneously; this is where brokers come into play.

As a medium of contact between you and the company, brokers act as mediators. For their service, they charge a commission. Many of the trades were carried out by traders in the early stages of the stock exchange industry on behalf of their clients. Nowadays, brokers don't perform transactions on behalf of their customers. Clients still have the opportunity to monitor their accounts quickly and efficiently. You will need to open the broker's account, and the broker will give you access to trade on that account.

Several software programs where you can transact directly in financial markets have been successfully implemented. The proposal and access credentials for the program will be provided by the brokerage firm you choose.

Tradable insurance is an option; you can buy or sell options from an official broker or pass them, much like a bond or stock, on an exchange. An option may give you the chance to maximize your cash. Still, it may be high risk (expiry date) because it expires eventually. Every options contract covers 100 shares, in the case of stock options.

An example of an alternative is if you want to buy a home for some reason but don't have cash available straight away, but you will get the cash next month. At the negotiated price, you can now buy the asset and sell it for a profit. Perhaps when the house has plumbing problems or other issues, the asset might also drop in value. You forfeit the contract's original investment when you decide not to buy the asset and let your purchase option expire.

Options trading works on this basic concept, but it is much more nuanced and requires more realistic risks.

**Assess the system and style of investment.**

Trading has its tactics, methods, and strategies. According to various people, different variables vary. What does well for other people might not work for you, and there are two other classes of investors. Aggressive people invest differently than cautious individuals. People who are not scared to take chances are utterly different from those who are methodical and keep things easy. It's not worse or better. That's just how you get it done.

There are two significant kinds of traders in the market:

**Active Investor:** Traders are also viewed as active buyers. For a long time, they have not kept on to options, and their interests lie in gaining from fluctuations in the rate. Trade a lot, and as much as you can.

**The Passive Investor:** Such investors are often related to as buy-and-hold owners. They are the opposites, exactly. They are interested in making the most of each option's profit and, therefore, do not trade. And they can trade them once or twice when they do.

Most individuals could find themselves at any point between those two groups. Some of them tend to be more assertive, while others are a little more cautious. It would strive to enhance the quality of all, and one would think it would be in the center; this is not always the case.

Aggressive people are anxious individuals. Patience is not, for them, a strength. So, in most situations, if you push them to trade conservatively, they do not even have the know-how, and for them learning it's not an option. The same thing goes for the conservative crowd; chaos in their mentality is generated by pressuring them to exchange more options than one or two.

By comparison, with just one objective at a time, conservative people are most relaxed, which encourages them to think directly and make the right options. This would be the ideal world, but unfortunately, there are still strings attached.

Even the most rational investor should have to move quickly and sell all his options should an emergency occur. An aggressive person should learn that, for whatever reason, there are instances where trading may be prevented, forbidden, or interrupted, and they can have to hold on to their options.

The more you get into trading Options, the smarter you will become. The market alone, sometimes even the hard way, will teach you regardless of what kind of investor you might be when it is right to catch on to an option or when it is time to sell it (i.e., it will set you back a great deal of money).

## 2.2 The Pricing Mechanism of Options Trading

You might have successfully turned the market by trading stocks following a diligent framework that envisions an excellent step up or down. Numerous traders have also built the confidence to make money in stocks by recognizing one or two good stocks offered to take a significant move soon. However, if you do not know how and when to reap the motion's benefits, you could be left high and dry. If it sounds like you, then it's time to begin exploring options.

This chapter will address the factors to consider if you plan to trade options to maximize the value of market fluctuations. Options are derivatives contracts giving the purchaser the right, but not the entire duty, to sell or purchase (in the event of a call) the associated asset or product at a fixed price (referred to as strike price) before the contract expires. The right comes with a charge, referred to as the option's premium. For trading options, knowing how to calculate the premium is substantial. It depends on the probability that only the right to sell or purchase would become valuable at expiry.

Before embarking on the field of trading options, investors should have a detailed awareness of the determinants that determine an option's investment potential. The expiry date, the intrinsic value, the current stock price, interest rates, volatility, and the cash dividends will be included.

**The Black-Scholes Model**

There are unique pricing frameworks for options that use these criteria to determine an option's fair value. Of all these, the Black-Scholes model is the most known one. Options are like any ordinary investment in specific ways; you have to consider what distinguishes their worth to use them effectively. Often commonly used are other models, including the binomial model as well as the trinomial model.

Let us start with the driving forces of an option's price: intrinsic value, current stock price, volatility, and time value or expiry date. The stock's current price is relatively straightforward. The downward or upward movement of the stock price has a similar, but not equal, effect on the option's price. If a stock's value rises, the more certain it is, the price of a call option will rise, and the put option's price will come down. If the stock price falls, the puts and calls' price is more likely to occur the other way around.

The Black Scholes methodology could be the most efficient options pricing strategy. The formula is obtained with the cumulative normally distributed probability distribution by multiplying the inventory price. Subsequently, from the original forecast of the resulting value, the NPV (net present value) of the price multifaceted by the cumulative normal distribution is deducted.

The mathematics of the equations that make up the Black Scholes formula can be challenging and frustrating. Interestingly, you don't need to know or even understand math to use Black-Scholes analysis in your techniques. Options traders and investors have access to several software programs for online options. Today, many trading sites have comprehensive analytical tools for options, providing indicators and databases that measure and value options for performance.

Furthermore, we will dive deeper into option pricing to explain what constitutes the foreign vs. intrinsic value, which is relatively simplistic.

**Intrinsic Value:**

Intrinsic value is the price that each option would be given if it were decided to exercise today. The intrinsic value is technically the price at which an option's stock price is beneficial or in-the-money at a market rate. If the strike option's price is not profitable concerning the stock price, the option is regarded as out of the money. If the impact price is equal to the market price, this option is considered at the cost.

Even if intrinsic value encompasses the link between a strike's price and the stock's actual price, it does not consider how long (and how little) the contract is called to expiry. The time remaining on an option affects the option's premium or benefit, which we shall discuss in the following chapters. In other words, the value intrinsic is the fraction of the value of an option that is neither lost nor affected by time.

The value of an option reflects the successful financial advantage resulting from the imminent use of the option. It is usually the option's lowest value. For options trading in cash or cash, there is no inherent value.

**Volatility:**

The time value of an option also relies heavily on the volatility the market expects to display before the end of the inventory. High volatility stocks are usually more likely to be profitable through expiration. As a result, as part of the option's premium, the time value is usually higher, covering the stock price's additional risk of moving over and ending in the money. For inventories that would not change much, the time value of the option would be reasonably low.

One of the metrics used for calculating volatile stocks is called beta. Beta tests inventory volatility compared to other significant markets. In general, volatile stocks have higher betas due to volatility in stock prices shortly before the option expires. However, high beta securities remain at higher risk compared with low beta stocks. Investors can gain substantial revenues from volatility, but volatility can result in severe losses as well.

The impact of volatility is the most complex and challenging to measure. Interestingly, many calculators are available to predict uncertainty. There are various types of uncertainty, including the most implicit and historical, making this much more fascinating. Statistical volatility or historical volatility is either referred to if investors in the past refer to volatility.

**Historical Volatility**

Historical volatility allows you to evaluate the potential extent of the future movements of the corresponding stock. Statistically, two-thirds of all stock price fluctuations occur over a fixed period, around more or less one standard deviation from the stock's shift. Historical volatility is reflected through time to show how unpredictable the market has become, enabling investors with options to make decisions on which exercise value is the most appropriate to choose for a particular strategy.

**Implied Volatility**

Implied volatility is precisely what the current stock prices imply and is used for theoretical frameworks. It helps specify an established option's current price and allows option strikers to evaluate a swap's viability. Implied volatility tests options markets would consider what potential volatility. Implied volatility is a measure of the prevailing sentiment of the market in that respect. This sentiment would be reflected in the option's price, allowing traders to assess the option's potential volatility and the stock, given the option's current price.

**Time Value:**
The time left has an options-related financial value called a time value because options contracts have limited time until they expire. The duration of an option before expiry and uncertainty or changes in the share price is linked explicitly to it.

The longer an option lasts, the better the chances that the money will end up in it. The time variable of an option quickly decreases. The actual interpretation of the time value is a fairly complex formula. As a general rule, an option would lose 1/3 of its cost in the first half of existence and 2/3 in the second half of its lifetime mostly. Securities investors must take this as an essential principle since the closer the option matures, the more necessary a change in the underlying security will impact the option price.

In other words, the value of the time is determined immediately following the cash flow between the price of both the stock and the selling price. As time value is the ratio of an option's intrinsic value, the time value is also related to an option's extrinsic value.

Time value is indeed the risk premium that the option seller needs to provide the option buyer with how stocks can be purchased or sold up to the option's expiry. The higher the risk, the greater the option's cost is, just like an option insurance premium.

## 2.3 Types of Options

The options classification system takes a step further than just using the method used to classify them for trading. The additional methods used to differentiate the various options are the underlying features they refer to and the expiration date. It extends individual outcomes to many types of options that exist across the universe. For an investor to understand the fundamentals of trading options, these options can be put forward. They are composed of:

**Call Options:**

Call Options are characterized by making available to a person the right to purchase the agreed asset on a date in the future. It seems that the purchased products have a value that is already agreed on. Some circumstances may make an individual make an investment call. The most popular scenario is when, after a specific time, one assumes that the asset will increase its value. A distinctive and unusual characteristic of calls is that they have an expiration date that depends on the agreement entered into by a person. The commodity that is being sought can also be acquired before the expiry date.

**Put Options:**

Puts are the absolute opposite of calls, as a rule. To the person who owns the put option, the right to sell the underlying assets is given. For the possible activities which have been allocated, the selling process appears to have a negotiated price. The situation appears during fascinating periods in the financial markets. An individual is likely to fall under set action when projected on the value of assets to fall. While being the opposite of the call, there are similarities between calls and puts. A significant joint occurrence is that each of them is limited by the time set. Consequently, places have an expiry date on the arrangement one has entered into.

**Cash Settled Options:**

These kinds of contracts are not distinguished by the actual transfer of the traded properties. What occurs in a cash-settled option may be related to the name it has. In this type of option, the income provided by the successful party is obtained in cash forms. Such variables influence this sort of trading options. If the asset being passed on is costly or difficult to transfer to the other party, it is about the case.

**European Style Options:**

People who are given these options are not allowed the same flexibility as those who use American-style contracts. The timeline is rigorous for this type of option. Only at the time of expiration and not before or after that date shall any person who uses contracts of a European type exchange his underlying properties.

**American Style Options:**

When it deepens down to options, the American style has little to do with purchasing and selling agreements. Following the terms set out in the contractual terms of the arrangement, it targets the lenses. Necessary knowledge at this level is that options come with an expiry date in their contracts, enabling a trader to buy or sell an underlying asset on the stock markets. Each person has the right to exercise his or her contract after the contract's expiry date in the American-style alternative. The described versatility seems to help a retailer using American style options.

**Exchange-Traded Options:**

For several financial market investors, these are also well recognized as listed options across the globe. It is related to as one of the most widely used kinds of options known to people. Contracts on public trading exchanges have several options that have been listed. Those are the types of options that are listed as currency trading options. They can be bought or sold by anyone with the aid of subtle traders.

**}Over the Counter Options:**

This kind of exchange option is traded mainly in the over-the-counter markets. These are traditionally standard features amplified by counter-trade options, making them unusual to the public. The conditions of the contracts of these types of options tend to be more complicated than the other options.

**Employee Stock Options:**

It is established that employees are presented with these types of stock options. The agency for which they operate as an employee or a particular company that offers the option will grant this contract. Its general use is to promote employee remuneration. It goes forward as the workers of a particular organization are given bonuses or perks. It has many benefits because it draws individuals to work with organizations that offer such services.

**Exotic Options:**

This is a concept that indicates contract options, which options traders have personally personalized. This tailoring's influence makes the contracts very difficult. They are called Non-Standardized Options in some cases. There are more peculiar arrangements available that are only present in the OTC markets (Over the Counter). In the current financial markets, some of these options contracts have begun to be expected. Such options include:

- Binary options: the holder of the corresponding financial assets must pay a fixed amount of money if the contract expires.
- Compound Options; the type of trading option in which the underlying financial asset is another option.
- Barrier Options: payment is often given before the contract price is surpassed to the holder of this contract form.
- Select Options: This options trading strategy helps a financial trader to determine whether to call or join at any time.

**Expiry-Based Options:**

As per their expiration dates, contracts may be differentiated in;

- Daily options, based on and defined by the cycles arranged in the exchange contracts. One is likely to have four months of expiry from which to choose in a financial year.

- Weekly Options, launched in 2005 and also referred to as Weekly Options. They have the specific qualities as traditional equivalents, of which they are assumed to have all the pacing. Weeklies tend to be used with restrictions on financial instruments.

- Quarterly options, found on financial markets with expiry dates equal to or close to fiscal quarters. Some people call them every week, and they terminate on the last day of expiration.

## Underlying Protection Options:

A stock option is a particular one that becomes the focus as individuals begin to think of options for trading. That is where, as a financial instrument, the related underlying assets may be publicly listed, and this is a simple understanding of individuals who have participated in this form of trade. There are many types of options involved in this scenario, including; A publicly listed company owns the stock options; the shares are generated; the underlying assets exchanged under this arrangement are generated.

- Basket option; this is a sort of trading approach with the underlying assets being several financial instruments.

- Future options; the futures contract is the underlying commodity used in this form of exchange to allow an investor to benefit from a future agreement. A future option often has a profit opportunity.

- Index options, which tend to be somewhat similar to stock options. However, there is one difference that depicts the blurred line. As stocks are not the corresponding type of protection being exchanged, separation takes place; separation takes place instead. For a company, they are the markers.

- Currency options; these arrangements vary drastically from other options. That is because the right to sell or buy currency is granted to a trader. Trade is made on signed contract terms.

- Commodity Option; Physical commodities tend to be the assets highlighted in this type of options trading.

**Some key pricing points to remember:**
- Options contracts can well be priced by using statistical formulas such as Binomial price or the Black-Scholes models.
- An option's cost consists mainly of two distinct components: its time value and its intrinsic value.
- Intrinsic value is just a measure of the attraction of an option that depends on the strike price vs. the stock's market price.
- The time value depends on the anticipated uncertainty of the underlying investment and the time until the option expires.

## 2.4 The Advantages and Disadvantages of Options Trading

As with any other financial instrument, options trading also comes with its fair share of advantages and disadvantages. To succeed in options trading, one must be aware of options trading's relative pros and cons.

**Options Trading Advantages:**

For options trading, lower initial capital commitment than stock trading is appropriate. The cost of an option (the premium and trading commission) is considerably lower than an investor's cost to pay directly to purchase shares.

Investors spend less money on the same sandbox but will earn it just like the investor that camped for the share if the trading goes their way.

There is a small limitation for option buyers. When you purchase an option put or call, you are not expected to track the trade. Suppose the time frame and direction of stocks are mistaken. In that case, your risks are limited to everything you have invested in the contract and trading charges. However, the downside maybe even more significant for options sellers; see the downside.

Options offer integrated versatility for traders. Investors may take specific strategic options before the end of an option contract, including:

- Exercise the option and purchase the shares to add to your trading portfolio.
- Exercise the option, buy the shares, and subsequently sell some or all of them.
- Sell the contract to another investor for "in the money."

When you offer the contract to another investor until it ends, some money invested in an "out of the money" option will theoretically return.

Options enable an investor to set an inventory price. Options contracts allow investors to freeze the stock price for a specified period to a dollar amount (a strike price) with an effort identical to the layover. It ensures that buyers can purchase or sell their shares at a strike price, depending on the type of option used, before the option contract expires.

**Options Trading Disadvantages:**

Options lead to unlimited / amplified risks for sellers. Unlike an option buyer, the option seller may bear much more losses than the contract price. Note that an investor may purchase or sell securities at a given price, even if the price is unfavorable, during the contract period (and there is no limit on how high a stock price may rise).

The investment thesis has little time to complete. The very essence of options is short term. Investors in options try to benefit from a short-term change in prices, which the trade should pay off in weeks or months, and this requires two correct options to make: the option of the best time to buy the contract and the determination, immediately before the option expires, of when to sell, exert or leave. Long-term equity holders have no deadline. You have sufficient time for years or even decades to allow your investment ideas to play.

Future traders must fulfill some requirements. You need to apply through your broker for authorization before even starting trading options. After you answer questions about your financial capital, investing experience, and the risk of trading options, the broker will assign you a level of trading to determine what kinds of options trading you are allowed to place. Any investor trading options must have a minimum deposit of $2,000 in his brokerage account, a valuable industry standard, and opportunity cost.

Trading options investors can incur additional costs that affect their profit and loss results. Some options trading strategies allow investors to set up an account with a margin, which is simply a loan line to leverage if the transaction goes against the loan. Each brokerage company has a different basis for opening a margin account, determining the amount of money and securities within the account and the amount and interest rate. In general, the interest rates on marginal loans may vary from one to the center of the range.

In the event of investors failing to make a loan (or a balance of a brokerage account falls below a certain amount due to regular fluctuations in the market), the lender of the money can apply for an invitation to make a margin and liquidate the investor's account if there is no more stock or cash allocated.

# Chapter 3: The Greeks of Options Trading

Now that we understand what drives the prices of options, we will make this more quantifiable, and this is accomplished using the so-called "Greeks," five parameters represented by Greek symbols (or letters) measuring how an option's price will change. You do not have to know precisely how they operate. Just what they say is that you can look them up to obtain their values at any given time. We begin to look at intrinsic value, i.e., how the option changes or varies with its underlying stock price.

Different factors that can either assist or harm traders based on the type of locations they have acquired can impact an option's price. Efficient traders recognize variables affecting the pricing of options, including 'Greeks,' several risk indicators named after Greek letters denoting them, indicating how vulnerable an option is to a decline in time value, changes in implied volatility, and price movements in its underlying security.

This can be a challenging attempt to anticipate what will happen as the market shifts to the value of a single option or a situation involving several options. Since an option's price does not always seem to be moving according to the underlying security value, analyzing the factors leading to an option's price action and its impact is critical.

Options traders also refer to Delta, Gamma, Vega, Theta, and Rho for their options positions. These terms are collectively referred to as the Greeks and provide measurable factors to calculate the vulnerability of an option's price. These words can sound daunting and overwhelming to novice options traders, but subdivided, the Greeks refer to fundamental principles that can help understand the danger and possible rewards of an option position.

## 3.1 Delta (Δ)

The first would be Delta, which tells you how the Option changes with its underlying stock price. We have stated earlier that there is no price shift of 1-1 concerning the stock at the option value. By focusing on Delta, you can see how it is going to change.

Firstly, we need to identify the call options. If the Delta is 0.46, if the total stock price rises by $1, the option price will rise by $0.46. If the Delta is 0.74, if the corresponding stock price has increased by $1, the option price will increase by $0.74.

Put Options get a negative delta, which means an inverse link between the Put Option and the stock price underpinning it. That is, if the price of the underlying stock falls, the value of the Put Option will increase, and if the price of the corresponding stock increases, the value of the relative Put Option will begin to fall.

Therefore, if the Delta is-0.26 and the underlying asset price increases by $1, Put Option's value will decrease by 26 cents. If, on the other hand, the total stock price had dropped by $1, the price of the Put Option would have risen by $0.26.

Delta is versatile, and the total amount will always be adjusted when any major variable changes the value options. Find an option with a $100 strike price on a stock valued at $102, with a 14-day bid period. In this scenario, the Call Option price is $2.48, and the Delta, in that case, is 0.75. The rate for the Put Option is $0.47, and the difference for the Put Option is-0.25. And if the stock price increases by $1, the Call Option is projected to rise to $2.48 + $0.75 = $3.23. The price of the respective Put Option will be $0.47-$0.25=$0.22.

It is just about what is going on. Still, since other aspects affect the price of options, the correlation is not reliable. The fact is that the option call increases to $3.84 and, as the options put it, reduces the price to $0.27.

We have also said it is complicated, and what follows when the share price rises by \$1 for both options is the delta rate. Now consider the call delta to be 0.84, but-0.16 for put.

That says something important to us, particularly that the higher the Delta, the more money in the stock.

Looking at that, we could see a lot of real options.

Provided that an IBM \$124 call is scheduled to expire on 6/28, it has a delta of 0.967. A \$139 call, which expires on 6/28, has a 0.5388 delta. The share price is \$139.20. So, there's more to your wallet for a \$124 call. The \$139 call is for money. We know that a second significant delta figure, a delta that is relatively close to 0.50, will be available for money options.

As the more cash you are in, the higher the Delta means that the money options will benefit (or be damaged) a \$1 shift in the underlying assets' price.

Another event that happens is that you get closer to the expiration; the higher the Delta is when the Option is in the wallet. If the underlying stock price remains at \$103, going from expiry to 7 days, the Delta will jump to 0.92 to show us a \$100 share price option. Moving to the 3-day expiry date, the Delta is 0.98. So, if you expect the stock price to change a lot in the next few days, having an option that will expire soon before the move happens could be a significant investment, look for incidents such as a call to profits or an indication of a purchase that might influence the price.

Note that the cash options have a delta of almost 0.50. The Delta for a call will be precisely 0.50 as you get close to maturity, and it will be-0.5 for a call if the money option is in. Buying money options can be difficult, so you are likely to have to opt for something similar.

If the Option is already out of the window, the lower Delta will be closer to the expiration dates. It can become remarkably thin a few weeks away from the Expiry Delta. A \$100 strike price, an option out of the money offer, a \$97 share value with three days to expire will have a 0.02 delta.

---

The Delta must sum the shortfall to 100 for the same place option (but note that it is represented negatively). In this case, if the price is $97, there will be a delta of-0.98, a put option with approximately the same terms, so a $100 strike price. In that case, it would have been worth $3.00, and if the corresponding share price had dropped to $96, the cost would have risen to $4. For putting, you can see the Delta increase to-1.00 and decrease to 0.00 for calling.

The price rose by $1 if the stock went the wrong way, then the Delta would drop to-0.92 for the put, and the put price would fall to $2.04.

The bottom line is that if the underlying stock price rises by $1, Delta should give you a quantitative approximation of how much the option price would change. The connection is direct, as this is a call option, and the Delta is represented as a positive number. In any given scenario of Put Options, the Delta is a negative number because the relationship is the opposite. And remember that if you take the actual delta value of the Set Option and compare it to the delta value of the Call Option with approximately the same strike value and the expiry date, it will add up to 1.0.

## 3.2 Gamma (Γ)

Gamma is a derivative of Delta, and this shows you how the Delta is changing itself. This is important because the Delta was complicated, we observed. However, emerging traders do not have to delve into this too thoroughly because you can test Gamma to see how much Delta can change if the underlying shares' price increases by $1. For both puts and calls, Gamma holds the same value. And if Gamma is 0.22 and Delta is 0.24 for a Call Option, and -0.76 for a Put Option of the same strike and expiry date, we will expect a $1 rise in the share price to trigger Delta to increase to 0.46 for the Option call. The position of Option Delta would change to -0.54. This is about what would happen, but remember if the Option changed the money delta values to 0.5 and -0.5, respectively.

Gamma describes the frequency of delta changes over time. Since delta variables change continuously with the value of the underlying protection, Gamma is often used to measure the movement rate and gives traders an indication of what to expect reasonably. For at-the-money options, Gamma's values are highest and lowest for those in or out of money.

While Delta varies depending on the underlying asset's value, Gamma is static, representing the delta shift frequency. This makes Gamma useful in calculating delta durability, determining an option's likelihood of hitting an expiring strike price.

Assume, for example, that two options have a similar delta value. One option has a high Gamma value, and another option appears to have a low Gamma value. The greater Gamma option will also have a higher risk, as an undesirable shift in the corresponding asset will have a minor impact. High Gamma value indicates that unforeseeable fluctuations tend to occur in an option, which would be bad for most traders searching for reliable prospects.

The simple way to display Gamma is to measure the reliability of a high probability option. Suppose Delta represents the probability that it will be in-the-money via expiration. In that case, Gamma shows the durability of that likelihood over time.

An option with such a higher Gamma and 0.75 deltas could be less likely than a lower Gamma option with almost the same Delta to expire in-the-money.

## 3.3 Theta ($\Theta$)

In the analysis of options among the Greeks, Theta is an important parameter. What Theta gives you details about is the Option's time decay. Theta is depicted as a negative figure, representing that the loss of time as it goes on causes the options' cost to decline.

Theta measures the level of time decay in the value of an option and its premium. The decay of time represents the degradation of an option's value due to the passage of time. As time passes, the likelihood of an option being lucrative or in-the-money decreases. When an option's expiry date gets near, the time decay begins to intensify as there is less time left to make an exchange profit.

For a specific option, since times go the same direction, Theta is always negative. Eventually, the countdown starts as an investor buys an option, and the price of an option begins to fall immediately before it expires, worthlessly, at the predetermined expiry date.

Theta is terrific for sellers and bad for buyers. A perfect way to visualize it is to picture an hourglass where the buyer would be on one side, and then the seller is from the other side. The buyer must decide whether or not to exercise the Option before the clock runs out. And in the meantime, the value flows to the vendor's half of the hourglass from the buyer's hand. The transition may not be swift, but it is a constant loss of value for the user.

The Theta variables are always negative for extended options. They have always had a zero-time value by expiration because time only moves in one course, and the time has run out when an option expires.

The Theta values are considered stable and streamlined over the long-term, but the slopes become steeper for at-the-money options as the expiry date passes. The extrinsic value of the in- and out-of-the-money options is relatively low towards expiration as the price likelihood matches, the strike price decreases.

Put it this way, there is a reduced chance of making a profit close to expiration as time is running out. At-the-money options may be much more likely to achieve these rates and make a profit, but the extrinsic value can be changed over a limited time if they do not.

Let's consider a few examples.

Suppose we have a call and have options in place, with three days to expire, at a strike price of $ 100. The call price is $1.20, and if the share price of the corresponding stock is $101, the put price is $0.20. For both the call and the put, the Theta is -0.073 in this case. That tells us that, when nothing else changes, each Option price will go down by $0.073. Call Option s is $1.20, while Put Option s is $0.20. We see the Call Option price falling to $1.12 and the price of the Put Option dropping to $0.12, shifting to 2 days before expiry and leaving all else the same, shifting almost precisely to what was planned. The Theta rose to -0.079 the next day, indicating that the closer you get to the Option's expiry date, the time decay happens more quickly.

Theta's twenty days to expiration is around half as high, with all else unchanged, at -0.035.

This is one of the essential truths of Options; that is, time decay occurs exponentially. The closest you get to expiration, the quicker the decay of time happens.

One of the factors that may make solutions appear confusing is the interdependence of all of these factors. So, imagine that, in 20 days, the stock price shot up to $108 to expire. In that case, Theta is down to -0.005. So, this is a mere 1/7th of the previous value. For the Putting Option, it decreases.

Likewise, Theta is proportional to the share price. And if the share price is higher, then Theta is lower. Consider a stock that has a $975 share price and a $1,000 strike price. In that case, Theta is -0.282 for the Option to call and -0.274 for the Option to call. That means that the Call Option price (which is $5.15 in this case) will drop by about $0.28 if a day passes and nothing else changes, and the cost of the Put Option will drop by about $0.27.

Here, the core principle is the same as previously; the time decay is a major fundamental one for pricing options. Test the Greek Theta to indicate that the Option price will decrease by the next day if all other goods are deemed equal.

## 3.4 Vega (ν)

The next Greek we shall find is Vega, which tells us the connection between the Option price and its implied volatility. Vega informs you how useful it is to adjust the Option's volatility. Generally speaking, a cash option is less vulnerable to implied volatility adjustments, while the cash option is more vulnerable to conditional volatility alterations. Generally speaking, Vega tells you how much the price of the Option will change if the variant shows 1% changes. Note that more volatility options are worth more money.

Vega calculates the likelihood of implied volatility variations or even the forward-looking estimated asset price volatility. Vega focuses on changes in the future volatility estimates while Delta measures actual price changes.

High volatility makes options very expensive since, at some point, the risk of hitting the strike price is more significant.

Vega tells us exactly how much the option price will increase or decrease, considering the rise or decrease in the amount of implied volatility. Optional gains of vendors from a drop in volatility, but it is the reverse for options investors.

The implied volatility on the entire market for options reflects price action is important to remember. If there are more buyers, option prices are offered to increase, and implied volatility will increase.

Long-range traders thrive on bid rates, and short-range traders profit from bid rates. This is why there are extended options with positive Vega and shorter options with a negative Vega.

Assume an equity stock price of 500 dollars per share, and 40 dollars is the strike price, ten days expiry, and 23.5% volatility. Vega, 0.285. A call is worth $13.73, and $3.69 with the same settings is evaluated. The call's price would be $14.02, and the put amount to $3.98 if the implied volatility was raised to 24.5 percent. In other terms, Vega tells you that with every point of implied uncertainty, the cost of options increases. The closer you hit the expiry date, the smaller the Vega becomes.

Vega is positive and negative for shorter positions when you are in long positions.

## 3.5 Rho (ρ)

Besides the Greek risk factors mentioned above, options traders can also consider other more complex factors. One example is Rho (p), which is the rate of change between an option's price and the rate of change of 1%. This tests the exposure rate.

Rho is a price stability measure against a change in the risk-free interest rate. As interest rates do not adjust much or so much these days, Rho is not given much attention. Rho would become a more critical parameter in a quickly evolving high-interest-rate world, as in the late 1970s.

Assume that a 0.05 rho and a $1.25 price appear to be the call option. If you raise interest rates by 1%, the call option's value will rise to $1.30, with all the others equal. In any case, the opposite is valid for put options. Rho is highest for options for money with long periods before expiry.

## 3.6 Important Key Points to Remember

Here are some essential key points related to risk evaluation in options trading using the options Greeks.

## Key Points about Delta:

- Delta appears to increase significantly closer to the expiry date for close and money options.
- Further, Delta is measured by Gamma, which would determine the shift frequency in Delta.
- Delta can also transform in response to implied shifts in volatility.

## Key Points about Gamma:

- Gamma seems to be the lowest for both deep-out-of-the-money and deep-in-the-money options.
- Gamma would be more significant when the Option gets close to the money.
- Gamma is positive for prolonged options and negative for short options.

## Key Points about Theta:

- If they carry greater implied volatility, for out-of-the-money options, Theta can be successful.
- Theta is usually the highest for at-the-money options because less time is needed to profit with a change in the underlying price.
- Theta will rise sharply because time decay speeds up over the last few weeks before expiring and can therefore dramatically undermine a long option holder's position, significantly if volatility decreases at the same time.

## Key Points about Vega:

- Vega will rise or decrease without price fluctuations of the underlying asset based on changes in implied volatility.
- Vega will increase in response to the alterations in the corresponding value.
- Vega drops as the Option gets nearer to expiration.

The Greeks allow traders to provide an essential indicator of the option position's risks and potential advantages. When you understand the basics, you will start to apply this to your current strategies. That's not enough to know just about the total capital at risk in an option position. To understand the probability of a trade producing profit, it is essential to analyze many risk-exposure metrics.

The Greeks help investors to determine how fragile a particular transaction is to price fluctuations, variations in volatility, and the passage of time, as circumstances change forever. It can carry the trading of options to some other dimension by combining the Greeks' appreciation with the risk graphs' useful insight.

Options are among the most potent instruments in the capital market. Their flexibility leverages the role of the trader to maximize returns. These products also allow consumers to deal with the threat by using them to hedge or benefit from the market's upward, downward, or sideways movements. Trading options bear a significant risk of loss, despite their many benefits, and are very volatile. Not everybody can grow into a profitable options trader. It requires a particular set of skills, personality traits, and mindset to be a successful trader of options, like any other financial field.

## 4.1 The Trader Mindset

The only thing that new traders are interested in is becoming wealthy. When their transactions are successful, they cheer, and they disdain money-losing trades. This is an awful idea here. The path to becoming an outstanding long-term trader includes recognition of why the trades have lost funds. Then it would minimize the number of trades that have crashed. In other words, when searching for other approaches, whether you buy a call or put options to see them disappear uselessly, then you will do better than buying options.

We all make deals that win and lose due to chance alone. Some relatively few traders are specialized in predicting the market direction. However, several other traders, including seasoned fund managers, have difficulty surpassing the market averages. Research findings have shown that most investors do not understand this fundamental concept, and they tend to believe that their predictions are smarter than their actual results. Put it this way, and they believe that they do better than ordinary earnings, although they do much worse.

Many skills are needed to trade effectively in the financial markets. They have the skills to determine the dynamics of a market and assess the course of a stock trend. But none of these technical skills are as crucial as the trader's mindset.

The components of what we would call trading psychology are emotional containment, quick thinking, and concentration. Find approaches that are well known to you. Use them when you think the market conditions are acceptable. Track the results. Find out how well it has become a fact of the market world you planned. You will discover the strategies work well over time, not only because the trading strategy itself was financially viable, but more precisely because you introduced it at the right time. Create continuity to take away those inevitable defeats. If the future leftover reward has become too small to justify the risk of obtaining the last few dimes on a contract, know when it is important enough and stop winning trades.

Gain knowledge of how it is possible to read maps. It takes a while, and it is never something that can be quickly mastered. Although there is no guarantee of outcomes, each edge contributes. If you get a purchase signal, then it's okay to get moving, even if you know the signal could be wrong. But success comes from reducing losses and learning all the metrics. Know which ones still work and which would not be more critical than even splitting. Study the results and gain an extra edge by knowing which strategy works for you.

Do not just exchange for trade. When your situation is complicated, take breaks from investing, but not from reviewing your results. If your tactics do not work, carefully decide whether now is the time to sit on the sidelines or follow another strategy. Do not just assume what you need to do, though. Make sure you have a practical reason for each trade.

If we have no specific skills when choosing our trade, we need to learn some skills that give us a trading edge. Without an edge, we would expect to win around half of the time. As investors, we can also do one of the two things when we take the cost of investment into account:

- Acquire a profit of over 50 percent of the total time;
- Make sure that we do not end up losing more money than we are earning from winning trades.

To achieve that aim, we need to practice good risk management and ensure that our risks are limited to acceptable levels. However, this is not the only thing that we can do to achieve success as an investor. The way we do stuff, the trader's attitude contributes significantly to almost any trader's potential course.

Traders must remain flexible and understand the routine practice. For example, you might take into account the use of options to mitigate risk. Experimentation is among the essential techniques that can be mastered by a trader. Experience can also contribute to psychological influences being reduced.

Traders should, eventually, periodically check their performances. In addition to assessing their success and particular positions, traders should reflect on how they have prepared for a trading season, how well educated they are on the markets, and how they are doing professional growth. This systematic analysis will help correct mistakes in trading, change bad habits, and improve overall returns.

## 4.2 Keep a Trading Journal

Trading journals allow traders to document their transactions and analyses throughout the day. Since a thorough journal includes details beyond only what you see in the brokerage statement, it is a powerful tool. This includes what market conditions are like and whether you have been interrupted or done anything wrong. You should also log the concepts of strategy that can occur when you deal with the day.

All investors can keep a trading log, but there is no time for day investors to spill their material on the paper regularly, and holding a trading log while operating can potentially prove counter-productive when the transaction occurs and results in missed trades.

There is, however, a straightforward solution that involves virtually no paperwork and gives you historical proof of the specific business circumstances you experienced on a particular day.

Get a screenshot to use. Instead of writing about market conditions, failures, what went well enough, and new plans and methods, take screenshots of the business day with specific typed notes.

Most investors mark up their graphs throughout the day, draw the lines and label signal levels to determine the pattern and find possible reversal points. The graph displays the exact market scenarios being traded. Intraday reports will clarify the market's understanding of the day, and in a trading journal, something words will never express well.

A picture is a convenient way to keep a trading journal, and yet you need to add some items to make it valuable when you look back at it for review.

At the end of the business day, take screenshots of your graph and paste them into an editing application. It would help if you had any of the above information in it. If you cannot see anything on one map, take three or four pictures and save them individually.

Please save the date every day as its file name and keep it in the trading folder saved on your mobile device or at an available location in the database. Develop subdirectories for each year and a quarter to make the files more readily detectable.

After a week or quarter, go back and assess how you performed, mention common problems, and identify your skills. These insights will help you take advantage of your strengths and show the areas you need to work on.

Capturing screenshots is much more productive to collect data than you would by writing in a paper anyway. If you prefer to write stuff down, you can also do it straight on your graphs or keep a handwritten trading log. Be diligent in this process so that you will have every transaction registered that you make.

## 4.3 Trade Using Buying and Selling Calls

A call option allows the user to acquire a certain amount: the cost of strikes, but never the obligation, within a specific time frame, an inventory, or any other form of financial instrument. A call option is commonly called a call. If the Option dealer wants to use his right to purchase, the purchaser must pay the protection. At a specific time before the specified expiration date, the holder can exercise the specific Option. The expiry date maybe three weeks, two months, or a year. The purchase cost is paid to the seller following the Option's strike price's closeness to the security rate at the Option acquisition time. In other words, the price depends upon the probability of unlikely exercise of the Option by the option owner before the end. Options are usually sold in 100-share batches.

If and when the cost of a good is increased to a more excellent price than an Option Strike price, an Option Call owner will profit. On the contrary, the call option seller anticipates a fall in the commodity price or hopes that the strike/exercise's price value will never exceed the exercise's value. In this event, the cash earned for the sale of the sum will be a real benefit. If the price for protection does not increase just above the strike price before it expires, and the law expires without profit, the Option would not be very advantageous for the holder to exercise the right. No more than the call option price would have been lost to the user. If a specific security price goes over and above the strike option's price, the investor can use that Option profitably.

For example, suppose that you have purchased an Option for 100 shares with a $30 strike option. The stock price rises from $28 to $40 before the Option expires. You could exercise your right to 30 dollars and buy 100 shares, giving you an instant 10 dollars per-share value. There will be 100 net profit shares, ten times the share, minus the already paid purchase price. If, in this case, you paid $300 for this call option, you would eventually get $700 (100 shares x $10 shares = $700) in a net benefit.

The purchase of calling options allows investors to commit little money to get a potential advantage from increasing the underlying security prices or preventing positions. Small investors make large profits from small capital quantities using options. On the other hand, corporate and institutional investors utilize options to increase their marginal profits and safeguard their stocks.

**Purchasing Call Option:**

The buyer is referred to as a call option holder. To increase the price above the strike price, the buyer buys an invitation option even before the expiry date. The benefit is commensurate with the deal, minus the cost of the attack, the premium, and all transaction costs associated with the sale. If the price is not slightly higher than the strike price, the buyer will not exercise the right. The customer would experience a loss equal to the premium for the Call Option. Assume, for instance, a $40 inventory of ABC Company and a $2 call-option contract with a strike price of $40 and an expiry of one month. With its strike $40 price, the investor hopes to raise the stock price and pay an ABC call option of $200. When ABC's share rises from $40 to $50, the buyer earns gross revenue of $1000 and a net income of $800.

**Selling Call Option:**
Vendors of call options also referred to as writers, offer call options hoping that the expiry date would be worthless. They paid for the premiums and made profits by pocketing them when the buyer successful and efficient use of its Option is the buyer's profit or net loss when the security price rises above the Option's strike price.

## 4.4 Use Tactics to Manage the Risks

Many people mistakenly believe that options are much riskier than stocks because they do not fully understand what options are or how they operate. Nevertheless, with, for example, a defensive position, options could be used to mitigate positions and minimize risk. In speculating on a stock going high or low, Options can be used, but with far less risk than buying or shortening the real equivalent of the underlying stock. The subject of this chapter in making directional bets will be these latter risk minimization options for use.

**Traditional Calculation Method of Risk:**
The common and standard way is the first approach to balancing the risk distinction. Let's go back to the subject and see how it all works: if you were to invest $10,000 in some $50 stock, you would get 200 shares. You could also buy two separate call option contracts instead of purchasing 200 shares. By purchasing the options, you pay less money and still have the same number of shares through management. The number of options is assessed by the number of shares that the investment capital could have acquired.

Say you are planning to buy 1,000 XYZ shares at $41.75 for a $41,750 profit. However, for ten call option contracts whose market price is $30 (in-the-money), instead of buying the stock at $41.75, you can pay $1.630 per deal. The purchasing options will incur a gross outlay of $16.300 in the capital for the ten calls. That is $25,450 in net savings or about 60% of what you will spend buying the shares.

It is possible to use the $25,450 savings in several ways. Firstly, it will take advantage of other possibilities to give you more diversification. Secondly, you can only stay in a trading account and collect prices in the money market. By interest aggregation, what has been called a synthetic dividend can be created. For example, if $25,450 is invested in a money market account, it receives 2 percent interest per year. The account will receive $509 interest a year for the deal's life period, equivalent to around $42 a month.

In a way, you are now receiving a dividend on a stock that does not pay one, even while profiting from the sale of options. Using approximately one-third of the funds available to purchase the stock directly, this can also be achieved.

**Alternative Calculation Method of Risk:**

The other risk-based alternative for managing the cost and scale the difference:

Buying $10,000 in stock is not the same as buying $10,000 in total risk options, as we have learned. Exposure options carry a much higher risk due to considerably increased loss potential. You should have a risk-equivalent option position concerning the stock position to level the field.

Let's start with the stock's position: buying 1,000 shares at $41.750, for a total investment of $41.75. As a risk-conscious investor, a conservative technique that market experts suggest, you are also entering a stop-loss order.

You maintain a stop order at a price, limiting your loss to 20% of the investment, which is $8.350. If you are willing to lose this amount, the amount will also be the amount you are ready to pay for an option position. In other words, you only need to spend $8,350 on risk equivalency purchasing choices. With the same dollar sum at risk as you were willing to lose in-stock position with this strategy, you are in the place of options.

If you have inventories, stop orders will not safeguard against gap openings. If the market opened for an options contract lower than the strike price, you have lost everything you could, i.e., the total cash you used to buy the calls. You can undergo a much more significant loss if you own stock so that the options' position becomes significantly less risky compared to the stock position.

Say you are buying a $60 biotech stock, and it breaks down at $20 when the company's medication kills a test patient. At $20, your stop order will be processed, meaning a devastating loss of $40. In this case, your stop order did not provide much protection.

However, you pass on the stock ownership and instead buy the call options for $11.50. As only the amount of money you paid is at risk, there is a dramatic change in the risk situation now. And if the stock opens at $20, $40 will be lost to your buddies who bought the stock, while you will only lose $11.50. The options are less hazardous than stocks when used in this way.

By deciding the correct amount of money to invest in a position on options, the investor can access the leverage intensity. The goal is to keep the accumulated risk balance, using risk tolerance as your guide to running a series of "what if" scenarios.

# Chapter 5: The Technical Analysis

When you trade, you will feel a variety of feelings, which is unpreventable. From the satisfaction of making a profitable deal to the disappointment of taking a loss, you will go through the full range of feelings. You will doubt your financial choices, maybe question why you have ever started trading in the first place, maybe even choosing to believe that you are at the height of trading and born to become a trader.

Anxiety and greed will be the two primary emotions driving your decision-making. It does not matter whether you are making your first trade or your hundredth. There would be no fleeing of uncertainty and greed.

Technical analysis works because everyone has to deal with anxiety and cynicism, which we can see from the statistics. Human tendencies do not alter, and only when you understand what they are can you start trading them.

## 5.1 Support and Resistance

The principles of support and resistance are two of the most widely debated features of technical analysis. Traders use these concepts to study chart patterns to relate to price points on graphs that appear to act as barriers, preventing an asset's value from moving in a specific direction.

At first, the definition and concept behind acknowledging these levels seem simple. Nevertheless, as you will figure out, support and resistance can come in various ways, and the principle is more challenging than it first seems to learn and practice.

Technical analysts utilize support and resistance levels to define price points on something like a graph where the odds favor a delay or reversing of a dominant trend. Support exists when a downwards trend is supposed to pause due to a saturation of demand.

The resistance exists when an uptrend is expected to stop momentarily due to supply saturation. Market psychology also plays an essential role as investors and traders understand the past and respond to changing situations to predict potential market changes. Support and resistance zones can be identified on graphs incorporating trend lines as well as moving averages.

A resistance level is a relative price that the stock cannot break beyond. The resistance level can be hit several times without even being able to break through into the stock. At these levels, you will discover that the sellers exceed the buyers and push the price downward.

A support level is the price level that will not be broken down by the stock. The support stage can be pushed several times without even being sufficient to smash through all the stock. The buyers dominate the sellers at sure of these levels and push the price upwards.

They are more and more frequently affected; support and rates of resistance are increased. You will see the price beginning to run until these levels are ultimately violated.

Support is a price point whereby a downtrend can be expected to stop due to a saturation of demand or purchase desire. As if the value of equity or shares decreases, the requirement for shares increases, thus creating the support line. Meanwhile, resistance regions appear due to selling activity as rates have risen.

Once an area or 'region' of support or resistance is already established, these price levels may serve as possible entry or exit points because as a price hits a level of support or resistance, it is capable of performing one of the two things: rebounding from the level of support or resistance, or breaching the level of price and moving along its path before approaching the next level of support or resistance.

The sequencing of individual exchanges is based on the assumption that there will be no assistance and resistance areas. Traders will "bet" on the path and can quickly decide if they are correct, whether the price is stopped or passes through by the level of support or resistance. It is possible to close the location at a small loss when the price falls in the opposite direction. However, the change can be significant if the price shifts in the right direction.

Many experienced traders will tell stories about how specific market prices appear to deter traders from moving to an underlying asset price on that particular path. For example, suppose that John maintained a stock position throughout January and August and expected the investment price to rise. Let's imagine that John knows that the price struggles to get above $39 multiple times over several weeks, although it has become very close to getting above that amount. Around $39 will be considered a resistance level by traders in this scenario. As these price levels reflect places where a market runs out of power, Resistance thresholds are often referred to as a cap.

Support refers to levels on a graph that seems to act as a basis by avoiding the downward movement of an asset's price. A purchase signal may also correlate with the ability to recognize a degree of support. Usually, this is the region where market investors see the value and continue to drive prices higher.

## 5.2 Momentum

Momentum is the level at which the price or volume of security rises, i.e., the rate at which the price shifts. Simply put, it reflects the rate of the shift in price changes for a particular asset and is generally represented as a rate. In technical research, momentum is called an oscillator and is used to help detect patterns.

**The Basics of Momentum Trading:**

Investors may use momentum as a trading strategy. Once a momentum trader recognizes progress in the stock price, income, or profits, the trader will always consider a long or short position in the stock to expect that the momentum will proceed either in an upward or downward trend. This strategy is based on short-term fluctuations in a stock's price rather than intrinsic value.

When introduced, an investor may buy or sell, depending on the intensity of the developments in an asset's value. If a trader intends to use a momentum-based approach, he maintains a long position in a stock or commodity that moves up. When the stock is steadily declining, he maintains a short position. Buying low, selling high, trading momentum tends to buy high and sell higher or buy-low-and-sell-lower instead of the conventional trading approach. Momentum investors concentrate on the pattern generated by the most recent price split instead of determining the trend of progression or reversal.

Think about it as the momentum of an engine. When a train starts, it accelerates but passes slowly. In the middle of the ride, it ceases to accelerate but moves at a more incredible speed. As it slows down, the train slows down at the end of the ride. For the momentum investor, the train trip's favorite aspect is in the center, as the train runs at its maximum velocity.

Momentum investors like to chase outcomes. They aim to attain alpha yields by investing in the stock market that trends one way or another. An efficient business is associated with trending-up stocks. Some are better than others, as measured by development over some time.

Some methods for momentum traders help to identify the trend, such as the trend line. A trend line is a line drawn from the high price towards the low price, or inversely, over a given period. If the line rises, the price goes up, and the buyer's momentum buys the stock. If the trend line falls, the trend falls, and the momentum investor sells the inventory.

A strictly technical measure in this way is momentum investing. While momentum may be related to basic performance metrics, such as sales and earnings, historical asset prices are most commonly used as a complex function.

**Potential consequences to Momentum Trading**

Just like every other trading technique, there are risks associated with momentum trading. It will help if you recognize that you use this strategy to bet on other market participants' interests, and price patterns are never secured. And be always alert for sudden reversals or changes that occur. This may happen due to unwelcome news or shifts in investor's confidence in the market.

Momentum is the frequency of acceleration in security price or intensity.

A trader will select a long or short stock position, hoping that its momentum will continue in the upward or backward trend.

Momentum trading takes place on the backs of others, and market trends are never guaranteed.

Investing momentum could be successful, but it may not be realistic for all stakeholders. The implementation of momentum investment would most likely lead, as an investor, to net portfolio losses. When you buy an increasing stock or sell a declining stock, you will respond to earlier reports than the experts at the momentum investment funds' top.

They will get out and leave the bag containing you and other unfortunate people. You will also have to be more mindful of the turnover costs and just how much your taxes will eat up if you happen to plan it right.

Momentum trading is not for everybody, but it can often lead to spectacular gains if done correctly. Trading in this style requires extreme discipline because the first form of failure must stop transactions, and the assets must be promptly placed in a new trade that shows power.

Variables such as fees have rendered this form of trading inefficient for many traders. Still, as low-cost traders take on a more prominent position in short-term active traders' trading professions, this story is increasingly shifting. The desirable objective of momentum traders is to buy high and sell higher, but this goal does not come even without a proper proportion of difficulties.

## 5.3 Financial Leverage

A concept used by investors as well as businesses is leverage. For investors, to try to optimize investment returns, the concept of leverage is being used. To use leverage, you have to take advantage of various instruments, such as futures margin accounts and options.

In Options Trading, the use of leverage helps maximize the earnings. Trading in options will give you enormous leverage and make it possible to produce big profits for a comparatively small investment.

Leverage is the possibility to trade a large variety of options with just a small amount of money. However, studies have shown that the risk for non-leveraged securities is about the same in leveraged options.

Trading options through leverage is usually assumed to be riskier as it exaggerates the potential of the firm. For instance, you can also use $500 to make a trade with a capacity of $7000. Know the first trading policy: do not exchange something that you do not want to lose.

This is not as straightforward as you believe it is; that is why you have to understand what you have been doing.

Leverage helps you to use money more productively. To this end, as it helps them go for more comprehensive positions with tight budgets, many traders favor the trade.

When you use leverage, you do not reduce the possible advantage you can gain; instead, you reduce specific trades' risk. For instance, if you want to invest your cash in 1,000 options at $7 per share, you would need to risk an investment of $7,000. It implies that the whole amount of $7,000 would be at risk. However, you may use leverage to put a smaller amount of cash, thereby reducing the risk of failure.

This is the approach you would need to take a look at leverage, which would be the perfect path.

Before you can exchange leverage, you should come up with a way to optimize each deal's gains.

**Here are a few useful tips that you can follow:**

You have to reduce your losses and then only allow your profitable trades to work successfully. Therefore, you need to know when and how to reduce your losses to not end up bankrupt, like how you make other trades. You need to start using stop losses when operating leverage in exchanges.

As an investor, you need to measure your stop-loss array not to end up losing more than you can pay for. At any given moment, the device you use will depend on the business situation. Always guarantee a set that guides you.

Most traders try to pursue a trade to the end, which inevitably discourages them and makes them lose a lot of cash. Until a move happens, you must agree and plan for the next opening. Always be careful because another one would probably come along, just like it was the last chance.

Instead of setting market limits, rather than saving on charges, pick small orders. The restriction orders also encourage you, when you trade, to rein in your feelings.

Consider making sure you understand technical analysis before you get into trading. Technical research will ensure that the information you need to make decisions quickly is accessible to you.

Using Leverage in Options Trading comes with its benefits and drawbacks.

**The Benefits:**

When you leverage and achieve more amazing trading performance, you increase your financial capacity as a trader. You can alter the amount of leverage by your professional judgment. That is also because, when you establish a trading account, you can regulate the amount of money you carry into a deal. The good news is that leverage can be used free of charge, but you need to know how it works and whether it will work for you or not.

The level of leverage continues to variate. Some trading platforms have leverage from as little as 1:1 up to and beyond 1:1000. As an investor, it is usually a smart idea that you go for the highest leverage possible to make the most substantial profit.

Another advantage will be that low leverage makes it possible for you as a new investor to succeed. When going out in options trading, you have the opportunity to make comparatively small trades with little to show for your efforts. With leverage, you can use leverage to position trades that span thousands of dollars without risking the same amount in terms of investment. As long as you know what you have been doing, you can enjoy tremendous profits.

**The Drawbacks:**

You may need to understand that leverage appears to come with many disadvantages, just as it is a perfect way to make immense profits.

With leverage, you would be threatened with huge losses if the trade tends to go in the other direction. And because the initial outlay is much less than what you end up losing, many traders underestimate the danger of putting their money at risk. Try to make sure that you are working with a ratio that helps protect your money and then understand how to deal with trade risk.

When you are using leverage to sell, you lose full ownership of the asset. For example, when you are using leverage, you give up the ability to enjoy dividends. This is because, regardless of trade status, the dividend sum is deducted from the portfolio.

A margin call is when the lender demands the transfer of funds from you, so you keep the trade free. You have to decide whether you want to add funds or exit a role to minimize exposure.

If you use leverage to sell options, you can buy the lending institution's cash to use the full position. Many traders prefer to keep their positions open overnight, attracting a premium for cost-covering.

It takes comprehensive knowledge of various aspects of financial concepts to know how and when to trade options. For many people, the lack of knowledge to use leverage appears to be the leading cause of losses.

In the end, many traders who settle for options lose money, research suggests. For both smaller and higher leverage, this typically takes place.

## Risks with High Leverage

Usually, the money for forming a contract is sourced from a brokerage in the trading of options. Even when you have the opportunity to borrow large sums to put on a contract, you will gain more if the exchange is decent.

A few years ago, traders were prepared to offer leverage of up to four hundred times the initial investment. However, rules and regulations have been set up, and you can only access 50 times whatever you have at present. For instance, if you have $1000, you can handle up to $50,000.

**Choosing sufficient leverage:**

You will need to look at different variables when choosing the sort of leverage that will work for you.

First, you have to start with lower amounts of leverage because the more you collect from loans, the more you need to pay back. Also, if you were to use stops to ensure that the money invested is safe, it would help. Remember, losses will not go down quickly.

All in all, the leverage that you think is convenient for you must be selected. If you are a professional, go for low leverage so that you mitigate risks. Then optimize your returns and go for maximum leverage if you know what you have been doing.

When the direction of the trade moves, using stops on request allows you to reduce losses. That's the only protection that you can have to make it in the company as a beginner. This is because both the exchanges will be known and how to put them while mitigating any losses that could arise.

**The Vulnerabilities Involved in Leverage Use**
Trading options come with a set of risks that you need to live with so that the gains can be reaped and losses can be minimized. Here are some threats and how they can be handled.

**Losing more than you've got**
This risk is implicit in options trading, primarily if you use leverage to make trades. This involves opening the exchange and producing a small portion of the initial charge, suggesting that the economy will be in charge of your fate. When it works alongside your prediction, you will gain more than just the deposit. Conversely, if the course moves, you will potentially lose even more than your initial amount, and you lose the spot.

When this takes place, you must have a plan in place to help mitigate the risk. You have to set a cap, in this case, so you can decide the exact sum at which the transaction can end so that you do not lose more than you can cope with.

**Unexpectedly Closing positions**
The money will be lost if positions close randomly. You need to have some cash to make the transactions open in the account. This aspect is called the margin, and if you do not have enough funds to support the margin, even the place will close.

To mitigate this and add funds as needed, it would be nice if you kept a close eye on the operating balances.

**Massive Unforeseen Gains or Losses**
The markets can turn out to be volatile, and when they do, you will need to act quickly. Prices move based on announcements or something like that on the market, which could be adjustments in an announcement, case, or in trader actions.

In addition to having stopped, which tells you whether or not to respond, it will be better to alert you about any upcoming movement.

**Orders Filled Erroneously In**

If you send orders to position trade to a broker, and the broker instead does the opposite. This is called slippage. Whenever this happens, make use of guaranteed stops to make sure you protect yourself from any slippage that can occur.

**Common Errors during Leverage Use**

You need to have a strategy to exchange efficiently, even with towing leverage. With many mistakes happening in a trade, you lose rather than profit because you do not have the correct strategies to succeed. Next, let's take a look at the top blunders you will make when trying to get them to the top.

**Leverage Perplexity**

Many rookies are unaware of leverage and then go ahead to exploit this feature, barely knowing the danger they are exposed to. To make it realistic for you, learn to leverage information and practice it. Understand what it is and then investigate the best ways to make use of it. Without having to make huge losses, you may need to know how much you can carry in.

**No Plan for Exit**

Much like stocks, you have to keep your emotions in check when trading options. It does not mean that your passion and your fear must be swallowed; you must have a plan that you can implement. Once you have a defined strategy, you need to stick to it to have something else to lead you to start healing when things don't go to your side. You have to have an exit plan, which proves that you know when and how to exit a trade.

**Inability to pursue new approaches**
You need to make sure that you test out a few different techniques based on the amount of trading you want to achieve. Even if it does not work for them, several traders get a single solution and then stick to it. When this happens, you are also compelled to go against the principles you set down. Keep being positive so that new trading strategies can be discovered for options that allow you to get even more from your trades.

## 5.4 Moving Averages

The moving average is a critical technical analysis technique that balances market data by producing a continuously updated average value. The average is measured over the period selected by the investor, such as ten days, ten minutes, three months, or any amount of time. There are drawbacks to incorporating a moving average and potential alternatives to moving average to use in your trading. Moving average methods are also popular and can be tailored according to any given timeline to satisfy both long-term traders and short-term investors.

An MA (Moving Average) is a commonly used technical indicator that helps smooth out price trends by filtering out all the 'disturbance' from random short-term market fluctuations.

Moving averages can be produced in several distinctive viewpoints, and various times for the average period can be used.

Classifying patterns and measuring levels of support and resistance are the most commonly known moving average implementations.

Any time asset prices leap across the moving averages, it can create a trading signal for technical traders.

Many technical investors use the characteristics of various technical indicators, such as moving averages, to assist forecast possible short-term momentum; however, these traders seldom fully grasp the ability of such instruments to identify support and resistance levels. A moving average is a continually changing string that helps smooth out previous price specifics while also enabling the trader to develop assistance and resistance. When the trend is growing, the asset prices seek support at the moving average and how much it acts as resistance while the trend is down.

Traders may use moving averages in many ways to forecast upward movements as price lines travel above a central moving average or exit transactions if the value falls below a moving average. It also creates degrees of "autonomous" support and resistance regardless of how the moving average has been used. Many traders can play with various time intervals in the moving averages to look for this specific mission's best.

A moving average decreases the level of difficulty on a price chart" Given the trajectory of the moving average, to attain a simple understanding of the direction the price is going. The price eventually moves up (or has recently been) if it is oriented up, tilted down, and the price moves down across the board, heading sideways, and the price is likely to be in a range."

A moving average can also perform its role as support or resistance. A moving average of fifty days, hundred days, or two hundred days will function in an upward trend as a support level. Because the average is just like a ground (support), the price eventually bounces off. In a downtrend, a moving average can function as resistance; the value hits the point like a ceiling and then starts to drop again.

In this way, the price will not necessarily "follow" the moving average. The price might run through it slightly or change its direction before reaching it.

The trend is up as an average guide if the value is only above the moving average. If either the price is just below the moving average, the trend is down. However, moving averages have different lengths, so an uptrend can be displayed by one MA (Moving Average), whereas another MA indicates a downtrend.

**Forms of the Moving Average:**

MA (Moving Average) can be measured in different ways. A 5-day Simple Moving Average (SMA) sums up the five constant closing prices and divides them by five to create a new average per day. Each average connected to the next forms a unilateral streaming line.

Another common type of moving average is the EMA (Exponential Moving Average). As more metrics are applied to the latest values, the calculation is more complicated. Suppose you show on the same graph a 20-day SMA and a 20-day EMA. In that case, you will find that the EMA responds more immediately to price changes due to the increased allocation of the latest price information

Charting programs and trading systems are used to perform the operations, so no human calculation must use a Moving Average.

Not one type of MA is better than the other. An EMA can operate well in the equity or stock market for a moment, and at other times, SMA can perform efficiently. The time frame chosen for MA may also play an essential role in its effectiveness (regardless of its type).

**Length of Moving Average:**

Standard Moving Average lengths include 10, 50, 100, and 200. These lengths can be extended to any index period, depending on the trader's time horizon (ten minutes, daily, weekly, and so on.).

The duration or length you choose for a moving average also called the "lookback period," will play an essential role in how successful it is.

An MA can respond to price fluctuations much faster than an MA with a long time looking back, including a short time frame. The 10-day moving average is more accurate in monitoring the total price than the 50-day moving average seems to be.

The 10-day can be an analytical advantage for a short-term trader because it matches the market more closely and produces less 'lag' than the longer-term moving average. A 50-day MA could be more valuable for a longer-term investor.

The time required by a moving average to indicate a probable reversal would be the lag. Remember that when the market value is well above the moving average, as a reliable rule, the trend is called. Depending on that MA, when the price comes down below that moving average, it indicates a possible reversal. A 10-day moving average can have far more "reversal" signs than a 50-day moving average.

There can be a moving average of any frequency: 16, 25, 90, etc. Adapting the moving average to offer more accurate signals from past data will help generate better potential signals.

**The Crossovers:**

Crossovers are one of the fundamental moving average techniques. The first form is a value crossover, and that is when the value passes higher or lower than the moving average to indicate a possible shift in the trend.

Another technique is to add two moving averages to a map: one bigger and one smaller. Whenever the shorter-term MA passes over the longer-term MA, it is a purchase sign, as it shows that the pattern is changing. This is also considered to be a "golden cross."

In the meantime, when the shorter-term moving average crosses just below the longer-term MA, it is indeed a selling signal because it means that the trend is going down. This is known as a "dead cross."

Moving averages are estimated based on statistics, and hardly anything is predictive concerning the estimation. Therefore, results utilizing moving averages will be spontaneous. At times, the market tends to value moving averages of support/resistance and trade signals, while at other times, these measures do not show appreciation.

One big concern is that if the price movement becomes bumpy, the value can shift backward and forward, creating several trend reversals or trade signals. When this occurs, it is better to step back or use another measure to explain the pattern. The same thing can happen with moving average crossovers when the MAs get mixed up over a long time, causing multiple losing trades.

Moving averages perform very well but adversely in rough or varying conditions in transparent trading environments. This problem can be solved momentarily by setting the period, although these issues are likely to arise at some point, regardless of the time frame selected for the moving average.

A moving average streamlines the price statistic by straightening it out and making one fluid line. This makes the pattern easy to see. Exponential moving averages react to price changes quicker than simple moving averages. In some situations, that might be beneficial, while in others, it may trigger confusing positives. Moving averages with a much smaller look back period (for example, one month) would also react faster than a more extended lookback period average to price fluctuations (5 months).

Moving average crossovers is a common strategy for both entrances and exits. MAs are also able to highlight areas of potential support or resistance. While this may seem predictive, moving averages for a certain period are often based on historical information and represent the average price.

Investing using a moving average or any strategy involves an investment portfolio with a stockbroker.

---

## 5.5 Trends

A trend is the general direction of travel of a market system or the value of a product. Trends are defined by trend lines or market action in technical analysis that illustrate when an uptrend's pricing strategy produces more powerful swing highs and more powerful swing lows, or lower swing lows and lower downward swing highs.
Most traders prefer to trade in much the same direction as a trend, while opponents try to acknowledge reversals and sometimes trade against the trend. Uptrends and downtrends happen in all markets, such as stocks, shares, and derivatives. Patterns also exist in statistics, such as when monthly economic data rises or decreases from quarter to quarter.

- A trend is the total trend of the value of a segment, metric, or asset.

- Uptrends are characterized by increasing data points, such as high swing highs and high swing lows.

- Downtrends, such as comparatively low swing lows and decreased swing highs, are described by dropping data points.

- Many traders have chosen to trade in much the same general area as the trend, hoping to benefit from continued development.

- Technical indicators, trend lines, and price action are all instruments that can help define the trend and alert when attempting to reverse it.

Traders can recognize a trend using different technical analysis types, namely trend lines, technical indicators, and price action. For example, although the RSI (Relative Strength Index) is intended at any specific moment to indicate the strength of the trend, trend lines can show the trajectory of a trend.

A total price rise characterizes an upward trend. Nothing goes straight up for a long time, but there will always be fluctuations; the average trajectory must be higher to be called an uptrend, however. The most recent swing falls, and the same holds must be above previous swing lows for swing highs. When this structure starts to break down, the upward trend could lose momentum or reverse into a downward trend. Downtrends are comprised of more significant swing drops and lower swing peaks.

Although the trend is up, traders may think it will continue until evidence pointing to the contrary is available. Such evidence could also include smaller swing lows or peaks, price breaks below a trend line, or technical indicators turning bearish. Although the trend is up, traders focus on buying, hoping to benefit from a steady rise in prices.

When the trend fails, traders concentrate more on selling, seeking to reduce losses or benefit from the fall in prices. Most downtrends reverse at some stage, so as the value continues to decline, more buyers begin to see the price as a steal and move in to buy. This could lead to the formation of an uptrend once again.

Patterns can also be used by investors built on fundamental research. In this study method, changes in sales, profits, or other business or economic metrics are analyzed. For example, fundamental analysts can look for patterns in return on equity and sales growth. If earnings have increased over a couple of weeks, this reflects a good trend. However, if earnings have decreased over the past four years, this reflects a downward trend.

A trendless phase is called the absence of a trend, such that there is no overall upward or downward change over some time.

**Use of trends:**

Trend lines connecting a higher or lower series are commonly agreed to recognize trends. The upswings that produce support thresholds for future market movements interconnect a series of higher lows. A lower height series is related to downstream trends that offer resistance to future price shifts. These trend lines indicate the general trend direction for resistance and support.

Although trend lines give excellent guidance, they still have to be updated. For instance, the price may fall below the trend during an upward trend, but the trend is not inherently over. The price will go below the trend and then start to rise. In this situation, the pattern will have to be redrawn to address the new price behavior.

The trend does not focus entirely on trend lines to determine the trend. Most experts also choose to analyze consumer dynamics and other technical metrics to determine more accurately whether a pattern ends or not. A downturn below the above instance trend line is not necessarily a sell indicator, although if the price falls below an earlier swing or the value measure is swinging, it could be bizarre.

Trend lines are a primary but effective method for technological research (analyzing market charts). They contribute to lighting the general course of stock price movement.

The trends are focused on the idea that a market or market is evolving into trends (up, down, and sideways). Once the trend is broken, rates can be expected to keep up.

Three timescales may be used to restrict Trends:

- Short term pattern
- The cumulative pattern in terms of time
- Long term pattern

No set time may be used to reflect these (days, weeks, months, etc.). It depends on the period to which you apply. For a short, intermediate, and permanent pattern, a six-month daily inventory diagram is distinct from a monthly diagram. Perhaps the most important thing is to use all three frames to explain the actions of the stock. Have you ever been able to drag a sail or float against the river tide? Both three-times frames can also be used to make sure that you can "swim with and not against the moment" You use anything and hardly do something, all the time and effort. Swimming against the current is not prudent unless there is an apparent reason. Okay, it's the same thing to trade against the theme. You can do it and get profits, but it is easier to take the same pattern to increase your chance to profit. See the short, medium, and long-term fluctuations to keep the stock market's overall direction in line.

The fundamental rule is that the pattern needs two points, and a third is the validity of the line (it is taken seriously). Ratings are the highs or lows of the market.

If more prices touch the threshold, the trend gets higher.

Three specific trends are available:

**Upward Trend:**

If the pace continues to increase, it uses an upward trend. By drawing an "up and right" line over price dropping, an upward pattern is created: be sure to strike the line more firmly than you want, but not all points on the line must be reversed. Although prices remain above the trend, the upward trend is considered uncontained. Bullish trading tactics and upward trend lines greatly complement each other.

**Side to Side Trend:**
A pattern is sometimes referred to as a trend from side to side. This is because two parallel price barriers fluctuated between stock markets. You create a horizontal line by price rises AND price reductions to construct a channel trend lines. The area between the two sides is called the canal. A pair of cost barriers link trend liner rates to illuminate tracks. The top edge is commonly considered the resistance level, and the bottom edge is known as the support level. Often traders make the error that a trend just adjusts when the stock price sinks below the present trend.

**Downward Trend:**
A downward trend is used as prices decline. You set a downward trend by drawing a straight line over price peaks. Any business activity is below the current trend. Make sure you have as much high a market as you can hit the line. As long as the prices stay below the trend, the downward trend is called unchanged. The most special supplements are bizarre market tactics and downward trends. Trends are used to chart trades to let you see how this wave is going.

## 5.6 Advantages of Technical Analysis

Technical analysis is studying stock prices and practically all related data compiled from them, such as cycles, trends, volume analysis, and statistics. Technical analysis has been used to predict market fluctuations and provide ways of trade entry and exit. If you are a new trader, here are some of the advantages of technical research.

**Generate All Recent Information:**

The current price reflects all currently known knowledge about a commodity. Although speculation can always flutter that the cost can fall like a stone or rise, the market value is ultimately the balance point for all data. The commodity begins shifting from buyers and sellers as traders and investors start moving from one edge to another, reflecting the current perceived value.

Suppose this is true because the value contortions on that graph track both observations and value comprehension; the only data we need now is a price graph. It tells you that more selling participation than buying publicity or buying appreciation than selling passion, respectively, does not require you to think about whether a market value is dropping or increasing.

This makes trading even more manageable because, with technical analysis, we concentrate on the price graph. Failure to scan for financial results or read recent economic news... Even so, this is all expressed in the price.

**Price Changes for Trends:**

If prices only twirled outrageously and randomly, making money would be challenging. While wild swings do take place, trends typically adjust overall prices. The market has a directional bias that gives traders an advantage, deciding when a trend is in place when it is not (called a sideways price, variety, or adjustment) and then a primary technical analysis when a trend is attempting to reverse.

Techniques that follow trends are the most profitable trading techniques used by investors. This means that the trend is dissociated. Then, resources are identified to go in a direction that is somewhat close to the trend, thereby capitalizing on the contextually skewed price movement.

Trends occur at various "degrees." For example, on the weekly or monthly graph, you might well have a long-term upswing, and then on shorter stretches, or even on the far-left side of the graph, you may have a downtrend.

Technical analysis is the preferred method for short-term investors. This recommends ways to schedule your transactions so that you do not waste time, and you can apply the strategies in various markets or timelines if you prefer. The technological analysis focuses on a value reflecting all the current information of a product, and the actual perceived value is the current price. Scientific analysis is often used to distinguish trending or non-trending periods. Eventually, technological research is used to spot trends and then exchange them since history often expresses itself across specific frameworks.

## Chapter 6: Options Trading Strategies

You will get stuff moving when you grasp the basics of trading options. If it applies to options trading strategies, you should have a company strategy. Only what makes you determine what kind of strategy to implement in your trading plan. Depending on your trading plan, you will choose to build a strategy that will lead you to meet your objectives.

Trading options stand the risk that they will fail. However, acknowledging what you do is, by definition, an essential element. Trading and investing can always be a threat; you need to view what you are doing clearly. The key to a consistent and significant edge in trading options is to develop a successful trading strategy and then execute a series of strategies to allow you to achieve it.

A large number of people care about positioning and calling stocks when it comes to trading options. Well, that is the start. The fundamentals of the trade you have to learn. You want to aim for a few of the techniques from there that will help you do very well in trade. You should look at measures and tactics based on your trading strategy to show that you perform well in trading options.

If you have read this book to help you start trading options, you will know more about the initial training you need and how to pick a broker. You will also get an intuitive understanding of trading levels and how it can affect your ability to use various strategies.

At this stage, it is the right time to start thinking about how you can exploit trade opportunities. You might know everything that is there to know about trading options. Even such information is only helpful if you can put it into action and find ways to make some money.

Although options trading is quite complicated, it will ultimately be realistic for anyone willing to spend time studying the subject. However, it is not enough to learn how to trade options alone; you need to know how to make money out of it. This needs hard work and dedication because finding the right opportunities and then making the right transactions will have to put in the necessary effort.

## 6.1 Covered Call

A covered call refers to a financial transaction where an equivalent amount of the required protection is kept by the owner selling call options. To do this, a trader holding a long position sells call options via an asset to create a revenue stream on the same bet. The investor's long position in the product is "cover" since it means that the vendor can move the shares if the buyer wants to use the call option. It is called a "buy-write" trade if, at the same time, the investor buys the stock and writes call options on that stock.

A protected call will be a common strategy for options used to make money in the pattern of options premiums.

An investor who holds a long position by investing then writes call options to execute a covered call on the same investment.

Those who want to hold the underlying asset for a long time use covered calls but do not expect a significant price increase in the short term.

This strategy is ideal for an investor who feels that the associated price will not alter much over the near term.

Covered calls are also a balanced strategy, meaning that the investor only expects a slight increase or decrease in the subsequent stock price for the written call contract's length. This technique is also used when a trader has an unbiased short-term view of the product and holds the asset longer for this reason. It has a short position via the option of earning revenue simultaneously from the premium.

If an individual intends to retain the associated stock for an even longer duration is reported and thus does not expect a significant price increase in the near term, they can produce income (premiums) for their portfolio when passing out the downturn.

The covered call's gross benefit is the counterpart of the short call contract's market price, minus the sale price of the corresponding stock, and including the premium paid.

The net loss is equal to the selling price of the related stock, less the premium paid.

A covered call works on a prolonged position as short-term leverage and allows investors to earn income through the premium earned for selling the option. However, the seller revokes stock gains if the price increases above the selling price of the option. They are also obliged to sell a hundred shares at the market price if the trader wishes to exercise the option (for every contract written).

A covered call method is not realistic for a positive or a very adverse investor. If a trader is bullish, they are typically better off by not selling the option and just retaining the stock. The option reduces the sale profit, reducing the net trade profit if the share price increases. Similarly, if an investor is bearish, they will be better off dumping the stock immediately because the premium received for selling a call option would do nothing to compensate the stock loss if the stock continues to drop.

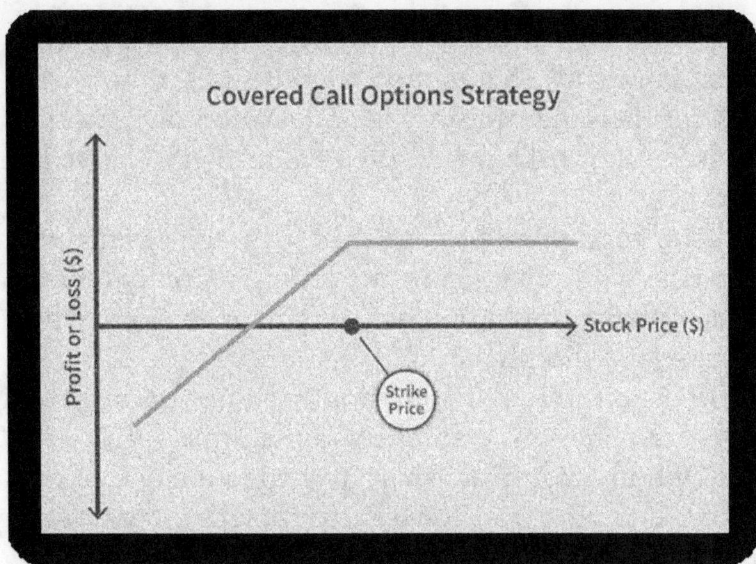



In the above graph of profit and loss (P&L), note that as the value tends to increase, the negative P&L is balanced by the position of long stocks through the call. Since the investor generates a gain from the sale of the call, their profit helps them sell their stock quickly at a level higher than the market price as the stock moves upward through the market price: the strike price including the premium received. The covered call's P&L graph looks quite a bit like a short, bare P&L graph.

## 6.2 Married Put

An investor buys a share in a married put approach, for example, company shares, and at the same time purchases options for the same stocks. The Put Option owner could sell the stocks at the strike rate, with a value of 100 shares in each contract.

An investor may choose to use such a strategy to maintain its market risk while managing a portfolio. Comparable to an insurance policy, this approach sets a price floor when the stock price falls sharply.

A married put refers to an approach to trading options whereby an investor purchases an equity ATM (At The Money Options) the same share to hedge a stock price drop while maintaining a long-term position on a given commodity.

The benefit is that the investor will, even in the worst case, lose a minimum but a limited amount of stock capital while still sharing in the profit of price growth. The downside is that the fee for the option is charged and is expected.

This options strategy will keep an investor from making an equity price drop significantly. The price of the option will make this solution prohibitive. The put options vary in price depending on the volatility of the associated stock. The strategy could be useful for low-volatility securities if traders fear that the price would change drastically.

A married set also functions in the same way as a customer insurance contract. An optimistic technique is applied when the investor is concerned about future short-term market risks. It also benefits the investors by keeping the shares in such a protective placement option, such as accumulating income and voting rights. However, while almost as positive as holding stocks, it does not offer the same advantage to get stocks by having a call option.

A married put and the long call have the same unlimited potential for profit as the associated stock's price growth has no limit. The profits remain lower even though they are offset by the fee or premiums of the option obtained only for holding stocks. When the supply increases with the premium charge for options, the breakthrough for the technology is achieved. The advantage over that amount is something.

A married put has the advantage that the stocks are now lower in value, and the future losses are reduced. The cornerstone is the difference between the item's value and the item's present value only if the married item has been purchased. Optionally, assume that the commodity at which the option is acquired will effectively be sold at the sales cost. In this case, the loss of the technique is confined to the fee for the option.

A married put is often referred to as a long synthetic call because they have the same gain pattern. The approach is similar to acquiring a standard (non-basic) call option as there's the same dynamic: minimal loss and infinite potential for gain. Precisely how much-reduced capital is required to buy a long call is the difference between those approaches.

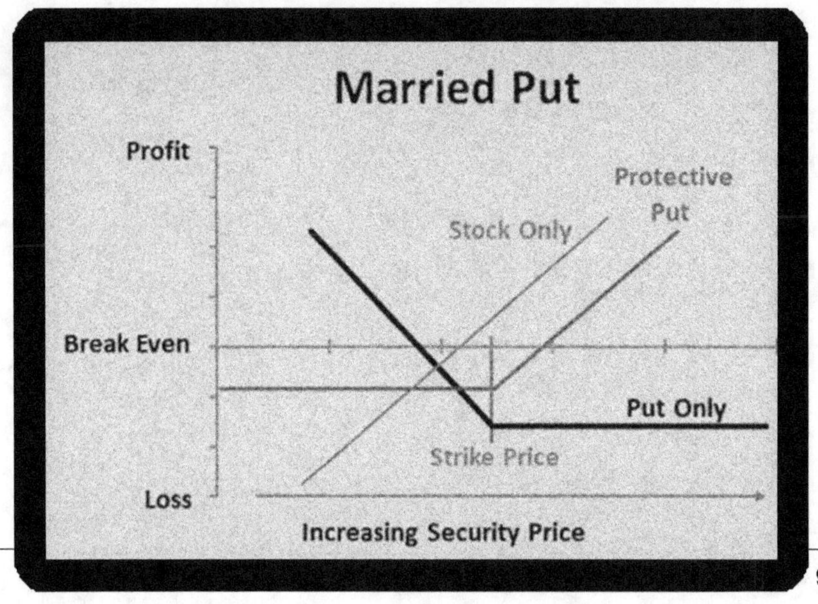

Only the long stock position in the graph above is the dotted line. With the long stock and long positions, the loss is minimized as the price falls. The stock can, however, be considerably higher than the premium expense. The married P&L graph appears similar to the long-run P&L graph.

## 6.3 Bull Call Spread

In a bull call spread technique, an investor simultaneously purchases calls at a specific strike price while still offering the same number of calls at a higher price. For both call options, there will be the same expiry date and underlying security. This form of spread strategy is mostly used and projects a modest increase in asset values whenever a trader is optimistic about the financial commodity. The investor can decrease its trade advantage by using this method while also decreasing the premiums spent (compared to buying a naked call option outright).

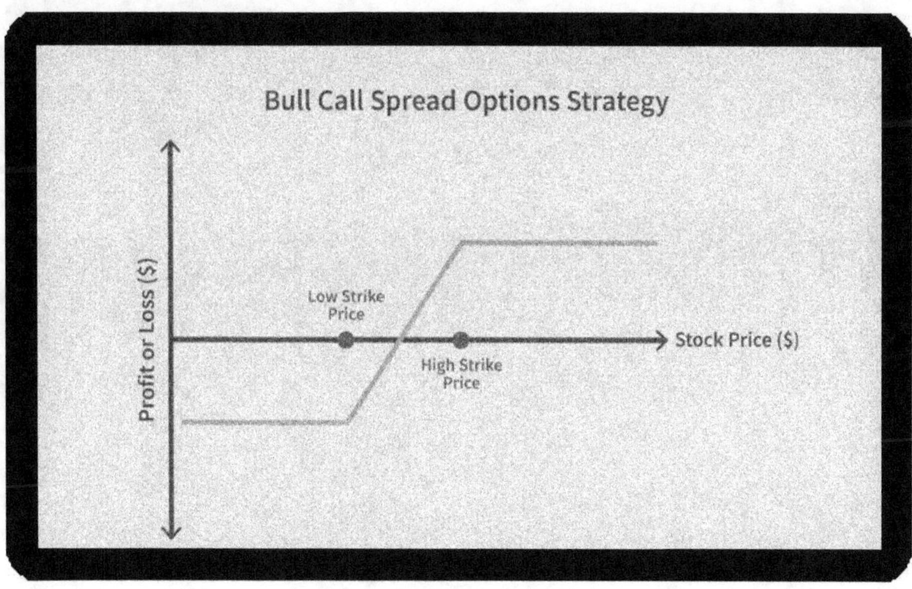

From the graph above, you will note that it is a promising approach. The trader appears to require the stock to appreciate an attempt to generate a profit on the transaction to implement this technique properly. The drawback of spreading a bull call is that you have little potential (even though the amount paid on the premium is reduced). Offering more significant strike calls with them is another way to cover the higher cost when clear calls are expensive. This is how a bull call is constructed for propagation.

## 6.4 Bear Put Spread

The bear-put spread approach is another kind of vertical spread. Simultaneously, the investor buys put options at a particular strike price in this method and sells the same puts at a lower price. All options are purchased to have the same expiry date for the same financial commodity. This method can be used when the investor has a bearish feeling about the financial product and expects the asset's price to decrease. The approach produces both limited losses and constrained gains.

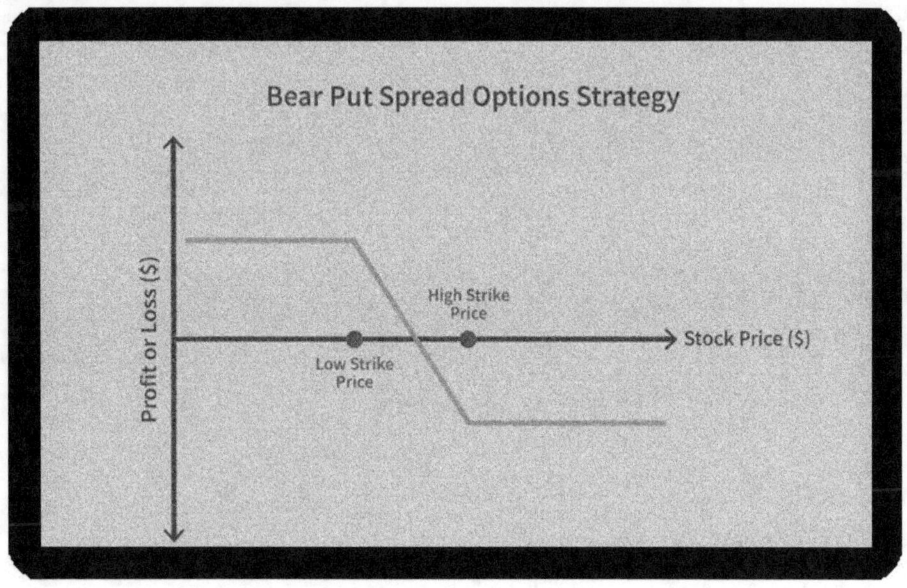

As shown in the graph above, you will notice that this is a pessimistic tactic. In return for this plan to be fully implemented, the stock price needs to collapse. While implementing a bear put spread, your profit is limited. The premiums invested are, however, minimized. If explicit puts are expensive, one way to recoup the high premium is to offer lower puts against them. This is how a spreading bear operates.

## 6.5 Straddles

A straddle is a neutral option technique involving the reciprocal acquisition of both a call option and a put option at much the same market rate and the same expiration date for the underlying assets when the value of the security increases or decreases from the market price by a sum more significant than the cumulative value of the premium charge.

A Straddle is a technique for options related to the purchase of both a call and a put option for the same expiry date and then the same strike price. The technique is financially viable only when the inventory rises or keeps dropping from the market price by more than the combined premium charge. It indicates what the expected uncertainty and trading scope of security could well be around the expiry date. Quite generally, straddle financing techniques refer to two different exchanges, covering the same underlying stock, with the two constituent exchanges being compensated by each other. Whenever investors expect a substantial change in the stock price, they prefer to use a straddle but are unsure if the value will rise or fall.

A straddle may provide an investor with two essential clues about the options market feels about some inventory. The first is the uncertainty that the sector anticipates from the protection. The second is the estimated trading scope of the stock up to the maturity date.

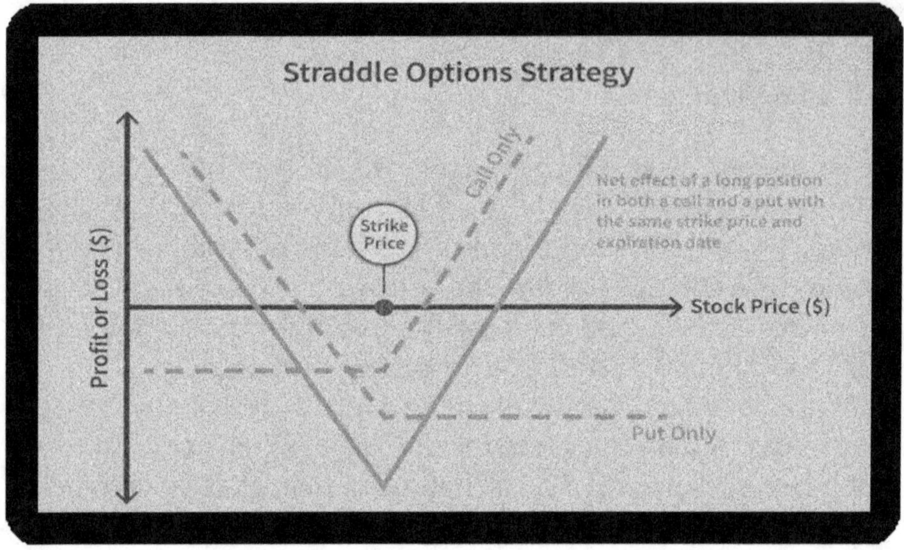


Note in the graph above how multiple break-even point points occur. This method will become financially viable when the product makes a big move through one route or another. The investor doesn't care what way the stock goes, only that it's a better shift than the investor charged for the total premium of the structure.

## 6.6 Strangles

A strangle is an option technique in which the investor owns a place with varying strike rates in both a put and a call option, with almost the same expiry date and financial instrument. If you assume that the underlying asset will undergo a significant price action in the immediate future but are not sure of the course, a stranglehold is an excellent approach. It is, however, profitable primarily if the investment fluctuates in price dramatically.

Except at varying strike rates, a strangle closely linked to a straddle uses alternatives, whereas a straddle uses a call and places it at a similar strike price.

In a long strangle, the trader simultaneously buys an OTM (Out of The Money) put and an OTM call option. The call option's market rate appears to be higher than the current selling price of the associated asset, whereas the put option's market price appears to be lower than the selling price of the asset. As if the call option potentially has infinite potential if the asset's value increases in value, this strategy has enormous prospects of benefit. Conversely, if the asset value falls, the put option will generate revenue. The risk for transactions is limited to the premium charged for the options.

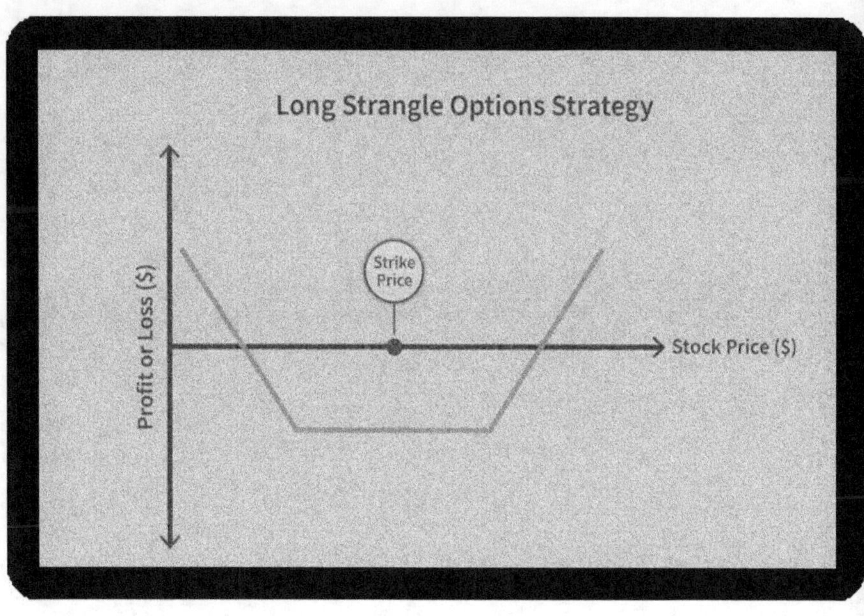

In the graph above, note how two break-even levels occur. This method becomes financially beneficial whenever the stock performs a massive shift in one direction or another. Again, whatever way the stock goes, it does not matter to the investor, just that it is indeed a better step than the total premium charged for the product by the investment.

# Chapter 7: The Common Mistakes and Tips from the Pros

There is no question that trading options offer the most enticing market opportunities to investors and traders. The opportunity to assert tremendous profits by investing minimal capital is one of the crucial reasons why options trading is becoming popular. However, although the potential exists for both, many investors cannot book revenue consistently and use options to produce wealth. As already mentioned, some fundamental pitfalls and errors contribute to the adverse outcomes of options traders. Trying to avoid such errors would provide the requisite advantage for any options trader. This chapter will discuss investors' most common errors during options trading and the experts' tips to have a perfect understanding of being a successful trader when you finish reading this book.

## 7.1 Common Mistakes in Options Trading

We are all creatures of behaviors and attitudes, so individual attitudes need to be shaken. At any point, Options traders seem to repeat the same mistakes repetitively. And the bad thing is, they should have avoided almost all of these errors neatly.

When selling options, it is possible to profit whether shares go upward, downward, or sideways. You can use option strategies to reduce losses, maintain earnings, and control large stock parts with a comparatively small cash outlay.

In a relatively brief time, you might also end up losing nearly as much as the entire amount you invested when selling options. That is why it is crucial to proceed with caution. Also, hopeful traders are likely to misjudge an opportunity and lose a great deal of cash.

This book aims to educate people on some of the most common trading mistakes to help options traders make smart choices.

**Not taking the possibilities and risks into account**

The marketplace does not always operate according to the trends shown by the stock market record. Some investors say that purchasing cheaper alternatives helps reduce losses by leveraging capital. Traders will over evaluate this form of protection by not following the guidelines for probabilities and possibilities. As a consequence, such a method could cause a significant setback. Odds define the probability that there will or will not be an occurrence.

Investors should remember that cheap options are often cheap for a reason. The option is priced following a mathematical estimation of the stock market's ability. The cost of an out-of-the-money (OTM) options contract depends heavily on its expiry date.

**Not Defining an Exit Strategy**

When trading options, as with when trading stocks, it is necessary to manage your impulses. That does not mean that you will need to have ice flowing through your arteries or that you are going to need to overcome your every doubt supernaturally.

It is a lot simpler than that; you should always have a strategy to work according to that plan and always work accordingly. And, no matter what your emotions tell you to do, do not diverge from it.

Organizing your escape is not just about minimizing losses on the opposing side if issues arise. And it would be best if you had an escape plan when a transaction is going your way. It is necessary to choose your upstream exit point and low exit point ahead of time.

Options are an asset that decreases over time. And the rate of decay speeds up as the expiration date gets closer. But if you call or location for a long time, and the shift you expected does not happen within the scheduled time frame, get out and move to another trade.

The truth of the matter is that you will have to have a strategy to get out of any trade, regardless of what kind of strategic plan you are undertaking or whether that is a success or a failure. Do not stick around because you are impatient with profitable trades or stay in failures for a reasonably long time because you expect the market to shift to your advantage eventually.

**Ignoring volatility**

Implied volatility measures the demand for a given commodity and forecasts long-term uncertainty. Whether implied volatility becomes relatively low or high is essential as it helps assess the premium paying value. Whether the premium is costly or inexpensive is vital to your viewpoint when deciding what alternative method makes sense.

When investing in cheap options, both novice and professional options traders will make fatal mistakes. Do not assume that cheaper options offer the same value as low-priced or low-priced options. Comparatively inexpensive options often provide the best chance of a 100 percent loss among all options.

Do your research before making bets on inexpensive options and stop paying odds on options trades. Expenses are much lower than they once were, so trading costs should be no concern.

**Choosing the False Timeline and Avoiding Sentiment Analysis**

An option with a more extended timeframe can usually cost more than a shorter duration. The stock has more time to move in the expected direction, though. Longer-dated replacements are less vulnerable to decay. A cheap front-month contract could, unfortunately, be daunting. Simultaneously, if the shares' movement does not meet the acquired option criteria, it can be catastrophic. For individual traders, managing stock activities over long periods is also emotionally challenging. Options' value can fluctuate dramatically as stocks pass through typical peaks and lows series.

A simple step in the right direction is to observe short interest, analyst ratings, and put activity. Financial business is never self-evident. It is intended to confuse a lot of the participants much of the time." It does not sound very motivating, but it opens up some possibilities for traders. If sentiment gets too extreme at one corner or another, gambling against the herd will generate huge revenues. Contrary interventions will help investors get an advantage, like the put/call ratio.

## 7.2 Tips from the Pros of Options Trading

It is a pervading misunderstanding of nuanced, risky options. However, the truth is that they are nothing more than a method to reveal securities in various ways. You see, classifying options as challenging to understand, but defining only a few basic options concepts makes them very beneficial and easily understandable. Anyone should learn how to trade options confidently.

Here are some helpful tips from the Options trading world for making your trading venture more straightforward and freer of possible losses.

**Be Diligent**

Great trades, bad trades, gaining trades, and failing trades occur. There will also be fantastic trades transforming to fail, and there will be horrible deals to gain. The trick is to realize that making good, substantial, sound deals is the highest likelihood of success. Perseverance is one position where stock traders and options traders should battle. They still feel a need to trade aggressively.

Much struggle is to describe the difference between effective and unsuccessful trade. Your percentage will increase before you focus on dealing smarter. Typically, the best hitters and options traders out there are not the most gifted; their advantage is that they focus their talents on specific, often lucrative trades.

**Defining risk strategies**

Established risk plans have a specified amount of money to risk. When we reach the market, this is understood. While we would like to minimize losses, specified risk transactions are not appropriate. What we used to minimize our losses is the approach's proven risk component.

We should do this for credit if we move or change losing trades. Rolling for loan increases the fee paid and boosts our breakeven point.

We must buy options on any options we have managed to sell due to the nature of complex risk strategies. This also makes turning for a loan impossible, and we'll never move for a debit.

Turning to debit is the complete opposite of turning to credit, removing the received premium, and even reducing your break price.

**Close your pre-expiry deals**

Options are dying properties, eventually expiring. Therefore, we seldom keep our trades expired. We are also out of preference for about 21 days before expiry.

You may feel that holding your positions through expiration is profitable as time decay is increasingly accelerating towards the expiry date so that you can gain faster. However, as expiration nears, fluctuations in options can increase as gamma increases. This rise in option prices is called gamma risk.

Excessive time decline is not deserving of the increased gamma risk in our investment strategies.

## Application of volatility

Implied volatility will be at the heart of our trial as options traders. The overstated nature of implied volatility is our trading edge's origin.

You must be careful to sell cheap options in low-implied volatility conditions. This may also be a time for methods that concentrate on increasing implied volatility. Schedule spreads, debit spreads, and diagonal spreads are methods that will positively affect an increase in implied volatility.

Nevertheless, in cases of elevated implied uncertainty, you want to be cautious buying expensive options. An environment of strongly implied uncertainty is one you want to sell expensive options. Credit spreads strangle, and iron condors include strategies to benefit from decreasing implied volatility.

## Reduce costs

Elimination of cost base can be achieved. The cost-based reduction will be when you sell an option to offset some of the costs against an inventory or options deal. This is likely as you limit your future profit in return for a high probability of gain.

Let's check an instance. Say you own $200 a share, and the market price is $200. Since stocks may either go down or up, this position has a 50/50 chance of winning. Let's say you are offering a $2.00 call option to stock. Your approximate shareholding is now $99, as you earn $2.00 in premium from the offered call option. The stock must now stay above $199 to make investors financially beneficial, raising the profit probability.

## Conclusion

The simplest and the most effective financial method to start dealing with is Options Trading; it gives you the freedom and flexibility you need and encourages you to get out of your 9 to 5 routine job.

As you have read the book now, you know that it is straightforward to exchange options, and there is no rocket science in it. You have no choice but to succeed in the company and the potential to make it in the trading world with the data collected in this book. You are now better suited to trade options through fundamental and technical analysis and other strategies. When they arise, you are also prepared to take on challenges and know what each trade entails from a technical perspective.

You know by now that to swap options, and you can use a good selection of instruments and pages. As the price of options continues to fluctuate from the start date to the maturity date, find a platform that suits your trading and growth needs. Bear in mind that each system has its strengths and drawbacks, so one that is 100 percent effective cannot be found. A stable platform is one that enables you to customize your experiences. Both novice and professional traders can operate such a platform. Since you will spend a substantial amount of time trying to grasp the advanced features and technology on the platform, a complex platform will impact your skills. Having the right instrument will ensure that you trade with bravery.

As you also know, it is not for everybody to invest in options, and not everyone can make money by trading options. To make one successful in the world of trading, and Options Trader needs to have many qualities. It is essential for a trader to be confident, alert, careful, and have significant control over his nerves.

Since options are incredibly unpredictable, you may lose all of your investment at once if you do not exercise caution. That is why you need specialized training like this one before venturing into it. As stock traders, a significant number of individuals who have succeeded in trading options started. Due to similarities between the two, you will have easy time trading options if you are already into stock trading.

**Patience and commitment, particularly options, are crucial when it comes to trading**.

You will be set up to be financially autonomous, to operate on your own and according to your timetable. To earn money, you will not have to stay in one position. You can raise money when you're on the go, knowing that all you need is an internet connection to work a few hours and set up your next trading plan.

We tried to give the reader all the most essential details and crucial insight into the Options Trading market in writing this book to help you achieve your goals.

After reading this book, if there is anything that we want you to know without a doubt, it is that you can achieve your financial independence by trading options and that there is no limit to the gains you can attain if you have the right knowledge and if you are ready to do what it takes to be a profitable trader.

Finally, it is essential to note that the shorter the trading time, the higher the tension and hazards involved. If you keep making your trades through the night, you have a chance of losing all your money and damaging your account. It is also fun for us that you have discovered a new way of raising capital from the stock market and have grasped all the features and skills you need to trade in binary options. Note that the theory is never accurate without implementation. If you need to get started, it is best to find a trading platform and put what you have learned into practice. Know that the more you practice, the more confident you become.

9 789564 028460